Piss-pots, printers and public opinion in eighteenth-century Dublin

Maynooth Studies in Local History

SERIES EDITOR Raymond Gillespie

This volume is one of six short books published in the Maynooth Studies in Local History series in 2009. Like their predecessors their aim is to explore aspects of the local experience of the Irish past. That local experience is not a simple chronicling of events that took place within a narrow set of administrative or geographically determined boundaries. Rather the local experience in the past encompasses all aspects of how local communities of people functioned from birth to death and from the pinnacle of the social order to its base. The study of the local past is as much about the recreation of mental worlds as about the reconstruction of physical ones. It tries to explore motives and meanings as well as the material context for people's beliefs. What held social groups together and what drove them apart are of equal interest and how consensus was achieved and differences managed can help to lay bare the lineaments of the local experience. The subject matter of these short books ranges widely from north Cork to the gypsum mines of Monaghan yet they have in common an exploration of different types of local societies. The world of Dublin with all its variations is revealed through an examination of one year in the life of the city (1707) and in another instance through one rather particular type of local world that was an important part of the make up of the city, the liberties. Again the reactions of the inhabitants of the city to an unflattering portrait of their world by one 18th-century traveller reveals how they discovered what they had in common in what is usually regarded as a period of division. Against this the violence associated with the murder of the Franks family in north Cork and the 1798 rebellion in Clonsilla reveal how local communities dealt with the stresses and strains of everyday life and how these could both be contained and explode into apparently random criminal activities. Despite these violent outbreaks, everyday life required the forging of alliances and understandings that allowed local societies to work. Understanding the shared assumptions that held communities together despite the tremendous pressures to which they were subjected is best done at the local level. Such communities remain the key to reconstructing how people, at many spatial and social levels, lived their lives in the past. Such research is at the forefront of Irish historical scholarship and these short books, together with the earlier titles in the series, represent some of the most innovative and exciting work being done in Irish history today. They provide models that others can use and adapt in their own studies of the local past. If these short books convey something of the enthusiasm and excitement that such studies can generate then they will have done their work well.

Maynooth Studies in Local History: Number 85

Piss-pots, printers and public opinion in eighteenth-century Dublin

Richard Twiss's *Tour in Ireland*

Martyn J. Powell

FOUR COURTS PRESS

Set in 10pt on 12pt Bembo by
Carrigboy Typesetting Services for
FOUR COURTS PRESS LTD
7 Malpas Street, Dublin 8, Ireland
e-mail: info@fourcourtspress.ie
http://www.fourcourtspress.ie
and in North America for
FOUR COURTS PRESS
c/o ISBS, 920 N.E. 58th Avenue, Suite 300, Portland, OR 97213.

© Martyn J. Powell 2009

ISBN 978–1–84682–193–6

Printed in England by
Athenaeum Press Ltd., Gateshead, Tyne & Wear.

Contents

Acknowledgments

My primary debt of thanks is to Toby Barnard who first suggested writing up my musings on Twiss as a book for the Maynooth series. He has been unstintingly generous with his time and knowledge and his comments on drafts have proven invaluable. Jimmy Kelly has been equally supportive of a variety of my projects and I would like to thank Raymond Gillespie for taking on Twiss and for his painstaking work with the final draft. Any errors and crudities – in style and content – that remain are my sole responsibility. The British Academy funded the research in Dublin and Manchester upon which much of this book is based, and I acknowledge the assistance and permissions granted by Teresa Bolger and Margaret Gowen & Co., the Bodleian Library, Bedfordshire Record Office, East Sussex Record Office, John Rylands Library and the National Library of Ireland. In addition the History seminar at TCD and the English seminar at QUB were excellent sounding boards for this material. Intellectual and social debts incurred during the writing of this book are legion, and those who have made Dublin, Belfast, Limerick and elsewhere such stimulating and convivial places to work include Nigel Aston, John Bergin, Michael Brown, Liam Chambers, Seán Donlan, David Fleming, Neal Garnham, Patrick Geoghegan, Ultán Gillen, Lisa Marie Griffith, Bob Harris, Moyra Haslett, David Hayton, Jennifer Kelly, Eoin Magennis, Anthony Malcomson, Ian McBride, Ivar McGrath, Shaun Regan and Patrick Walsh. The history department at Aberystwyth remains a very supportive environment, and I would like to express my continued appreciation for my colleagues and students there. As always my parents Roy and Eunice have shown pride and interest in my historical endeavours. But this book is dedicated to Laura, fittingly so, as she was forced to endure Swift's 'Strephon and Chloe' at our wedding.

1. Richard Twiss's *A tour in Ireland in 1775*

On 22 March 1773 Frederick Robinson, brother of Lord Grantham, Britain's ambassador in Madrid, offered his sister Anne the following description of a soon to be famous visitor:

> [Y]our friend Mr Twiss dined with me yesterday, you was much in the right when you said he was a great vulgar & you might have added a compleat gigg, it seems he is a great traveler, speaks most of the modern languages, & is the son of a man of considerable fortune, this at least is his own account of himself, the first thing he told us was that he had passed a day at Saltram with Mrs Parker last Autumn. by your account, I think it did not appear that he stay'd to dinner, he has produced no letter from any body to my Brother, Lisbon was the last place he came from & Mr Walpole gave him a letter to Monro. So much we know of his life, his character speaks for itself, & his education by his own confession has been rather neglected.[1]

Richard Twiss, aspiring tourist, was not, it is abundantly clear, a hit with the British diplomatic circle in Spain. Much of this spite can of course be put down to class prejudice. Twiss was no gentleman – in either sense of the word. His father made his money in commerce, and he was failing to adopt the niceties of 18th-century polite conversation. His exaggeration and braggadocio were sneered at by Robinson, and give credence to a memoir in the *Hibernian Magazine* which noted that 'his conduct was generally absurd, his manners gross, and his temper petulant and self-conceited.'[2] It is also clear that Twiss had failed to follow the rules of 18th-century touring. Just as a middling-sort mediocrity needed to be presented to a gentleman, so the tourist, before embarking upon his trip, was expected to secure sufficient letters of introduction to the great and the good in a particular country. After all it was the great and the good who were the guardians of the country estates and town houses, descriptions of which punctuated any tour worth its salt. Twiss then was short of these letters, and those he had were wheedled out of chance connections. A puffed-up day with Mrs Parker was offered as a vouchsafe to Robinson, while Lord Grantham in Madrid did not even merit that little condescension. Therefore the process of writing *Travels through Portugal and Spain in 1772 and 1773* failed to garner Twiss many friends amongst the English aristocratic set in the Iberian peninsula. Such an impression did not bode well for his next tour – planned for Ireland in 1775. The prickly peers and gentry of Ireland, very much aware of their second-class quasi-colonial status, would not be an easy audience to please.

Ill-equipped therefore, Twiss arrived in Ireland as one of an increasing number of semi-professional tourists who occupied their time and supplemented their incomes as travel writers. Following a lengthy sojourn in their country of choice these literary adepts would publish an account of their travels, commenting upon architecture, cultural pursuits, flora and fauna, and the manners and morals of the local inhabitants. As a consequence of a shift away from the Grand Tour – rendered less attractive due to European military conflict, as well as shifts in taste – towards the Home Tour, Ireland would welcome a number of these tourists in the second half of the 18th century. It was exotic, but accessible, wild, and yet tameable; indeed travellers may have had its effective governance in mind.[3] Notable visitors to Ireland included agricultural expert Arthur Young, the Frenchman De Latocnaye, and serial travel writers like Twiss and Sir John Carr. Twiss was the son of an English merchant based in the Netherlands, and thanks to his inheritance he became a travel writer of some renown. By his own reckoning he had covered more than 27,000 miles travelling on land, and had made sixteen sea voyages by 1775.[4] In April 1775 he published his *Travels through Portugal and Spain*, criticized in the *Monthly Review* for utilizing extensive quotations from other authors.[5] His sententious *A tour in Ireland in 1775* followed in 1776, and in 1793 came *A trip to Paris in July and August 1792*, which was, according to David Rivers' literary encyclopaedia of 1798, 'as usual, volatile but, for the greater part, sensible'.[6]

Twiss was by no means in the first division of 18th-century English writers. Rivers commented: 'Though not deficient in ingenuity and good sense, Mr Twiss belongs to the class of *petit maitres* in literature.'[7] But his abilities were not unappreciated in his lifetime, and he was elected a fellow of the Royal Society in 1774, with Benjamin Franklin and the musicologist Charles Burney featuring among his sponsors. Samuel Johnson said that he was enjoying reading his book on Spain – in his words 'as good as the first book of travels you will take up' – though not to such an extent that he could be bothered to separate the uncut pages.[8] A German work on gypsies cited Twiss's Spanish findings on this community in a respectful fashion, as did the *New London Magazine*. Subscribers to his *Miscellanies* published in 1805 included the Prince of Wales, Mrs Inchbald, Matthew Gregory Lewis and Joseph Banks. Although Twiss's visit secured the author a notoriety that resonated in Ireland, and beyond, well into the 19th century, there were three Irish subscribers, Richard Brinsley Sheridan and the Rigg sisters living in Derry and Clones. Maria Edgeworth also gave Twiss some little crumb of comfort by referring to him in her novel *Belinda* as an expert on Spain and chess.[9] The latter was one of a number of non-travel related interests, which also included toys and botany.

Richard Twiss's *A tour in Ireland* was written with the intention to both provoke and amuse. He had scored a minor success with his book on Portugal and Spain, but a follow-up was not a guaranteed success, and one wonders whether Twiss deliberately set out to outrage Irish opinion in the hope of selling a few more copies. It was nevertheless a serious attack on Irish society; barbed comments being directed at Ireland's cultural development and notions of politeness. Twiss provocatively observed that 'nothing is to be expected in making a tour of Ireland, beyond the beauties of nature, a few modern-antiquities, and the ignorance and poverty of the lower class of the inhabitants'.[10] In the two most notorious passages in his book, Twiss attacked the populace of Connacht, whom he dismissed as 'a kind of savages', and suggested that in terms of natural history the only remarkable aspect of the 'Irish species' was 'the thickness of their legs, especially those of the plebian females'.[11]

Following the ground-breaking work of John Harrington, Andrew Hadfield and John McVeagh, historians are beginning to pay attention to the importance and usefulness of Irish tours. In terms of interest in the 18th century, Glen Hooper devotes one chapter to 18th-century tourists in his *Travel writing and Ireland 1760–1860*. But this, and work by Joep Leerssen, Martin Ryle and William H.A. Williams, suggests that, as with the tourists themselves, Irish landscape and scenery are a more attractive proposition than burrowing into the underworld of Ireland's urban life.[12] In contrast this study is interested in a Dublin conscious of its urban development and an Ireland delighting in its print culture and political progress. The storm of protest following the publication of Twiss's tour has yet to be examined in any detail by historians. Paul Hyland and James Kelly have offered a brief commentary on a copy of *A tour in Ireland* annotated by Twiss himself. More recently Rachel Finnegan has published a new edition of the tour with an insightful introductory essay,[13] although the focus is upon the tour itself, rather than the way in which it energized patriotic print and political culture in the second half of 1776.

This short book therefore seeks to redress this neglect, focusing upon the backlash by a politicized Irish, and especially local Dublin, public opinion. It will place Twiss's book in the context of the other major 18th-century Irish tours before examining the role of printers and publishers in the controversy. In the spirit of a study that focuses upon the commercial and the urban over the rural and picturesque, subsequent chapters will consider Twiss's comments on Irish town and cultural life, and then the consumer product enthusiastically embraced by Ireland in 1776: the Twiss-pot. In the final chapter I will endeavour to offer some thoughts on the ways in which the anti-Twiss reaction reveals shifts in the nature of 18th-century Protestant Irish identity. Ultimately it will show that Irish and particularly Dublin print culture built up and then fanned the fire of anti-Twiss radicalism, but that its very artificiality – of target, response, coalition, even political climate – ensured that there were strict limitations on any shift towards 'national' unity.

The locus of this episode was the summer and autumn of 1776. In the months immediately following publication of the odious tour, the Irish patriotic press, dominated by the *Hibernian Journal* and the *Freeman's Journal*, printed numerous squibs and satirical articles all with the aim of excoriating Richard Twiss. Commentary also appeared in provincial newspapers such as the *Belfast News-Letter*, *Finn's Leinster Journal*, the *Limerick Chronicle*, and the *Londonderry Journal*, as well as newspapers more sensitive to government pressure like *Faulkner's Dublin Journal* and *Saunder's News-Letter*, and the monthly periodicals *Walker's Hibernian Magazine* and *Exshaw's Gentleman and London Magazine*; though it is clear that in the Irish newspaper world authorial integrity was as unimportant as in its English counterpart, and thus there was much cutting and pasting of articles. In addition a quick-thinking entrepreneur seized the opportunity to make some money out of the episode and fabricated a chamber pot with a picture of Twiss's face printed inside. This became the much-celebrated motif of the episode.

The unforgiving response to Twiss by the Irish local populace offers a revealing insight into the nature of Irish society in the late 18th century. Twiss's arrival came at a key point in the development of Irish patriotic politics. At the close of Viceroy Harcourt's administration, the British government had every right to look at the reinvigorated system of Irish government with some satisfaction. Lord Townshend had downgraded the role of the undertakers – prominent Irish landowners who undertook to facilitate the passage of government bills in the Irish parliament in return for a share of patronage – and his successor, Lord Harcourt, an experienced diplomat, had combined a more sensitive approach to Ireland's premier politicians with the lavish distribution of patronage, and secured not only a Commons resolution against the American colonists, but also the services of that doyen of Irish patriot politics, Henry Flood. Yet when the less talented Lord Buckinghamshire took over the reins of government in 1776 there were signs of parliamentary instability and a new lease of life for Irish patriotism. The imposition of a trade embargo in that year added impetus to calls for the relaxation of British restrictions on Irish trade. The polarization of Irish politics following the outbreak of the American War of Independence forged a tight-knit group of independent patriotic politicians, rendered more sizeable by the General Election of 1776, which had a new leader in the form of Henry Grattan. Outside of parliament this group was supported by societies like the Gleeg Club, the Free Citizens of Dublin and the Block and Axe Club, and by the patriotic press. In the summer and autumn of 1776 there were signs therefore of a rejuvenated Dublin public opinion. In many ways the assertive administrations of Townshend and Harcourt had played a key role in encouraging a more bullish proto-nationalistic mentality. The American war allowed this to flourish and Irish Protestant self-confidence was at its apex over the next seven years, which would see the rapid growth of the paramilitary arm of the patriot movement, the Volunteers, the concession of Free Trade, legislative independence, a renunciation bill by the British government and the passing of two Catholic relief acts.

2. Irish tours and tourists

In September 1775 the Scottish publisher John Murray advised a prospective travel writer John Gillies to pen a certain type of travelogue:

> You will find your account more I think in observing manners and customs than in giving insipid details of Pictures and Buildings. I own the latter should not be entirely neglected; but your work ... will be so much more valuable if you illustrate the former. This too gives more scope to Genius and Philosophy.[1]

The word 'valuable' is noteworthy, as this type of tour was ultimately of much greater pecuniary worth to a publisher than a soporific stroll around the sublime and the beautiful; at least that was the case until a Romantic vision firmly replaced its more earthy Augustan counterpart. Twiss, like Murray, was well aware of his readers' tastes. Hence we have a tour that is part essay on national character and part spiteful city guide, with a brief nod to the one thing that all visitors to Ireland could agree upon: Ireland had some rather attractive, if unkempt, scenery. The ingredients – particularly as many were filched from other chefs – were unlikely to inspire paeans of praise, but they created a storm of publicity. The likes of Twiss must have been in the Irish writer Thomas Newenham's mind when he bemoaned the rise of 'hasty, splenetic or fastidious tourists', who collected 'anecdotes, bon mots, or repartees', and offered them alongside 'elaborate descriptions of the lake and river scenery of Ireland'.[2] Arthur Young cynically observed that '[t]he present age is much too idle to buy books that will not banish l'enuye from a single hour. Success depends on amusement.'[3] For Newenham such travellers were only intent on 'reimbursing themselves for the expenses of travelling; well aware that works, which promise amusement to the idle and superficial, will be purchased with avidity'.[4]

If Twiss has any kind of modern legacy it is thanks to the hostile reception, and consequent high sales figures, of this book. Controversy – up to a point – was a gift to Twiss, and those involved in publishing his works. Indeed although it is certain that Twiss caused genuine hurt and outrage, and played a part in the development of Irish patriotic politics, it is also clear that this was a controversy stoked up – if not manufactured – by Ireland's printers. It was already clear that the Irish market for the written word had a pronounced patriotic flavour. Sales of the *Edinburgh Magazine and Review* had fallen after it printed a harsh review of Thomas Leland's *History of Ireland*, published in 1773.[5]

Consumers acted in this case without any serious encouragement from the Irish press. Could they, however, be persuaded to do the opposite to what might seem natural, and buy a product that was purposefully unpalatable to a patriotic Irish citizen?

In this light it is worth entertaining the notion that Twiss's tour was fabricated; a cut and paste job. After all, the so-called 'fireside travellers', or as the author John Bush termed them, 'garret-riders', were well known in 18th-century Britain.[6] Tours of Ireland with substantial elements of plagiarism were published in this period. In the most blatant example Philip Luckombe helped himself to substantial sections from William Chetwood's *A tour through Ireland. By two English gentlemen*, Thomas Campbell's *A philosophical survey of the south of Ireland*, Bush's *Hibernia curiosa* and Twiss's easily identifiable tour.[7] Luckombe's volume reappeared in 1788 as *The compleat Irish traveller* – possibly pirated without his knowledge.[8] Another example saw Mark Elstob meet no one of note on his *Trip to Kilkenny*, published in 1779, and this work also owed much to Twiss's tour; something that clearly irritated the latter as he cut out the offending sections on newspapers, cabins, modes of travel, fondness for potatoes and boiled eggs, ploughing techniques and Dublin's bay and its churches and pasted them into his personal copy of *A tour in Ireland*.[9] Reviewers and readers may not have been entirely unfazed by the practice, as an early 19th-century satire began a section with the words, 'Here is a rare opportunity for writing a chapter with my scissars.'[10]

Mark Elstob sought to assuage critics by acknowledging his debt to Twiss: 'if at any time I chance to run into Mr Twiss's track, which I believe I cannot possibly avoid, I hope you will forgive me.' Where Elstob felt disinclined to pilfer he simply recommended that his readers see Twiss's book for appropriate descriptions; as was the case on sculpture, architecture and painting. Elsewhere, he quoted extensively from Twiss on the Whiteboys.[11] Other tours contained obvious errors. Luckombe referred to Ireland's defunct lords justices, probably because they were still present when his unsuspecting source was writing. John Carr's tour placed the equestrian statue of George II, not in Dublin but in Cork.[12] It is not such a leap to presume that these individuals had never set foot in Ireland.

Twiss had certainly read Bush's *Hibernia curiosa* and Dublin-born Samuel Derrick's *Letters written from Leverpoole*, and some of his descriptive passages echoed the former. This in itself was unremarkable as tourists usually consulted other guides before embarking on their travels. Yet in a genre that had a shifting relationship with originality his tour was nonetheless marked out as something of an oddity.[13] Around a third of the book was made up of quotations from other sources, and, as with his Spanish travelogue, this was spotted: he was undone by unusual touristic candour. An Irish commentator noted of his Spanish tour that 'above one fourth of it was made up with quotations from

other writers, which were, indeed, the most agreeable parts.'[14] Also referring
to his Spanish book, Grantham's chaplain Robert Darley Waddilove,
commented on Twiss's claim that 'all the plates are executed after his own
sketches & such subjects as have never before been published', and then
provided chapter and verse on the true artists; only allowing one composition
to be Twiss's own.[15] A much-printed fake obituary of Twiss claimed that the
Latin poem that had secured his membership of the Royal Society had actually
been bought from a college servitor. Limerick publisher John Ferrar
complained of his Irish tour that 'whenever he has given a few lines of just
description, they are stolen verbatim from some other book.'[16] Elsewhere the
writer Richard Lewis noted the tendency of tourists to 'Paint Scenes they
never saw, nor e'er shall see', and another Irish poet referred to Twiss's magpie
eloquence.[17]

    As we have seen, Twiss had difficulties with letters of recommendation when
he visited Spain. There is no doubt that this could be a sensitive issue, and they
were frequently mentioned by tourists. Arthur Young proudly listed those who
had provided him with letters in his introduction, including Lords Shelburne
and Kenmare, Edmund Burke and Samuel Whitbread.[18] Charles Topham
Bowden referred to his letter of introduction from Edmund Burke to Colonel
Sharman.[19] De Latocnaye had a letter to the viceroy, Lord Camden. More akin
to Twiss, however, was Samuel Derrick who though carrying letters to Lord
Shannon, found that the earl of Cork had forgotten to mention his name. There
were, it seems, different classes of tourists. Without introductions to the great
and the good tourists had to make do with the second tier, or improvise.
Derrick was mostly in middling-sort company: he was entertained by a
contractor in Cork, and a banker in Clonmel, who was persuaded to write a
letter to a merchant in Waterford.[20] Richard Pococke had aristocratic
acquaintances, but his entertainment by military men early in his tour resulted
in a flood of similar invitations.[21]

    With one exception Twiss did not appear to stay, or visit, anyone of rank;
in stark contrast to, say, the Revd J. Burrows, who spent time with Sir Lucius
O'Brien, Nathaniel Clements and Edmund Sexton Pery, and Bowden, who
also provided fulsome detail on such matters. One Irish commentator later
claimed that Twiss 'was honoured with letters of recommendation to several
of the nobility', though then cast aspersions on the manner in which these
were procured.[22] A satirical card in the *Hibernian Journal* had Twiss himself refer
to 'those he visited without the Ceremony of Invitation'.[23] John Ferrar noted
an unconventional approach to accessing the tables of the wealthy, 'where he
had frequently introduced himself', particularly his 'manner of coming late to
gentlemen's houses, calling for wine, sitting up all night muddling by himself'.[24]
Perhaps his failure to name noble names came from a sense of discomfort or
embarrassment. Both the archbishop of Tuam and an anonymous peer were

said to have asked him to leave as a result of his conduct towards female members of the company.[25]

The only individuals that Twiss claimed to meet whilst in Ireland were men involved in the Dublin print trade: Sir James Caldwell and George Faulkner. Twiss had a letter of recommendation to Faulkner, provided by Samuel Johnson, who also gave Twiss an introduction to the author Thomas Leland; the insecure tourist would, in 1788, paste a copy of a letter from Johnson to Hester Thrale confirming this into his personal copy of his tour.[26] When Twiss arrived in Ireland, Faulkner was said, admittedly by a rather unreliable source, to have taken him around Dublin in his own carriage.[27] Twiss wrote that he stayed with Caldwell for a week, and although there is no direct reference to this in Caldwell's letterbooks, he must have mentioned Twiss in a letter to James Fortescue, MP for Co. Louth. Fortescue, in Swalinbar, replied: 'I received your letter and Mr Twiss was here but universally disliked'.[28] According to the tour Twiss had indeed visited this small spa town, and had complained that 'the accommodations are very indifferent'.[29] In his correspondence with his friend the antiquarian Francis Douce, Twiss mentioned meeting his own relatives whilst in Killarney.[30] They are not referred to in the tour, though he did spend eight or nine days there, again noting in respect of its two inns that that 'their accommodations are very indifferent'.[31] Happily at the outset we are at least able to prove that Twiss visited Ireland.

The Fortescue–Caldwell letter also proves that Twiss had made something of a nuisance of himself whilst in Ireland, and that the many poems and squibs that later appeared accusing Twiss of impolite behaviour had some basis in truth. His annotated copy of the tour reveals him to be smug, boastful and an inveterate name-dropper, and his personal correspondence is equally unflattering. Twiss was overbearing, pompous and condescending to his friends. Francis Douce was on the receiving end of hectoring letters demanding translations and comments on Twiss's publications.[32] Even after the Irish response, Twiss was rather brazen, seeing himself sometimes as manly wit, and sometimes as the wounded party. In his personal copy he appended a mocking rhyme by the poet Sir Charles Hanbury Williams to his comments on the thickness of female legs: 'nature indeed denies them sense but grants them legs, and impudence which beats all understanding'. In the same work he annotated his Fynes Morison quote on some rather lubricious female corn-grinding with the words: 'I won a wager of a Dozen of Port-wine by printing this anecdote'.[33]

These clippings and jottings in his own copy of the tour were selected either to prove that tourists were of the same mind as him, some going as far as using the same words, or, to justify his conduct in Ireland, through the inclusion of any vainglorious evidence he could find. Much of the former material focused upon Elstob, but Luckombe and De Lactocnaye were also employed. In addition he took the opportunity to quarrel with his critics, pasting their views along with his own rebuttals. As for braggadocio we have details of the Irish, German and Swiss editions of his Spanish tour; extracts from English newspapers; advertisements for his books, and quotes from positive periodical reviews. He even updated his own travel mileage figures, and number of voyages.[34] There was name-dropping aplenty, including luminaries from Johnson's Literary Club. Joseph Banks made an appearance, and we have the aforementioned Johnson–Thrale correspondence, proving that the great man of English letters had circulated his book, and had written letters of recommendation, and that Thrale wanted to frame one of his Spanish pictures. Not that these connections necessarily liked him. David Garrick, name-dropped in *Travels through Portugal and Spain*, reputedly responded to a tall-Twiss-tale of a church a mile-and-a-half long in Spain with the question: 'how broad was it?' When Twiss answered, 'About ten yards', Garrick addressed the assembled group with the witty rejoinder: 'This is, you will observe, gentlemen, ... not a round lie, but differs from his other stories, which are generally as broad as they are long.'[35]

Post-Twiss tour writers had to reflect carefully upon the impact made by the most infamous member of their fraternity. Twiss's sales were considerably better than Samuel Derrick's publication of 1767, which had been backed by Dublin's leading printer, George Faulkner. Should they follow his route into notoriety and high sales figures? Or was the popular outcry sufficiently alarming to ensure circumspection? Arthur Young pondered: 'I am perplex'd about the publication of my Tour, I do not want to make it an object of literary profit but I wish not to be a considerable loser by it.'[36] Young, always a more serious-minded author – 'a sensible writer' said Bowden – with many more influential Irish connections than Twiss and his ilk, followed an uncontroversial course and his tour was recognized by other tourists as having genuine instructional value.[37] Yet Twiss's tour had put Irishmen on their guard. John Foster, MP for Co. Louth and later Speaker, was underwhelmed by Young, and gave the impression that this was a common view in the county: 'he disappointed every one – he went with the rapidity of an express, asked for answers to a set of questions and seemed not to notice any thing else.' Foster had been led to believe that he was 'very ignorant, not communicative' and paid 'equal regard to the assertions of all persons'. In which case he expected that the tour 'when published, will be as bad as Twiss's'. Arthur Young was no ordinary tourist, and Foster had his own agenda, as he hoped 'to have got a deal of information from him'.[38] Even so, Young's determination to reassure his Irish friends that his experience of Ireland had been different was probably sensible. He wrote to Caldwell: 'It is not easy for me to tell you how much pleasure I experienced in passing through Ireland. I like the country, and love the people, so much indeed that I should have no objection if I could do it with any advantage of settling there.'[39]

Most writers achieving good sales figures for Irish books already had at least one tour under their belt, so literary fame of the right kind was important. Tours were not always easy books to hawk to publishers in the late 18th century, and Young's successful *Political arithmetic* of 1774, translated into several languages, seemed to count for little. Some London publishers ensured that they had a number of tours in their catalogue post-Twiss; but they were of a certain type. George Kearsley of Fleet Street sold Twiss's tour, and an anonymous Irish follow up, marketed alongside tours to France and the Netherlands, was full of the same kind of bile.[40] Sir John Carr's tour was written with English sales figures in mind. William Williams suggests that Thomas Campbell opted to market his *Philosophical survey* as the work of an anonymous Englishman on the grounds that an Anglo-Irish author would have been a less attractive proposition to readers. Campbell himself recollected: 'for what could be more absurd than for an Irishman, professedly, to write his travels in his own country';[41] though no doubt it was a better way of promoting Ireland's commercial needs, and perhaps also reflected his fondness for the persona of a polite Englishman abroad.[42] A decade later Richard Lewis had trouble with his Dublin city guide, it resting with a bookseller for almost a year-and-a-half before he gave up and published it himself.[43] Twiss opted to self-publish his *Travels through Portugal and Spain*, and despite its success this was the mode that he pursued with his Irish tour. Arthur Young complained to Caldwell: 'I am told the Dublin Booksellers give very little for the copy but that may be because I do not know the right persons, and as to a subscription the difficulties of that would I suppose be equal'.

He was perfectly correct in that supposition, and connections in the Dublin print world were undoubtedly important for a book to succeed in Ireland. Was it more than a coincidence that the two individuals whom Twiss explicitly mentioned visiting (excepting Lord Kenmare whose boat he borrowed) were men of the print trade? When persuaded of the virtues of subscription by his friends, Young asked Caldwell to distribute subscription receipts and requested the name of a likely individual in Ballyshannon who could receive subscriptions.[44] However he eventually warned his subscribers in Ireland that he would not publish, due to some of their number not being forthcoming with the promised financial support.[45] Ultimately the problem with a subscription was that it was a tactic that relied upon the author possessing a degree of fame. George Parker's subscription for his British tour was assisted by connections in the theatrical world.[46] Twiss looked to subscription for a later work, but he too became frustrated, and after a quarrel with a subscriber to his *Miscellanies* in March 1805 he lamented: 'I never published a book by subscription before (*and never shall again*)'.[47]

Until Union, and the need to sell its success, a very particular type of travelogue was presented; and its leitmotif was British superiority. A good deal of the typical tourist's time was spent in discussing existing preconceptions, and then, more often than not, reinforcing them; which was probably what much of the audience wanted. A check-list can be made of the sights and scenes that tourists must have planned to discuss, even down to comparisons and metaphors. Dublin bay had to be compared to the bay of Naples, as in Burrows, Elstob, Bowden, Clarke and Carr; the two were also juxtaposed in Twiss, and, typically, Dublin bay was labelled 'inferior'.[48] Another favourite was to liken Mallow to Bristol hotwells.[49] Around Ireland the beauties of Killarney had to be noted,[50] along with Cork's slaughterhouses, Kilkenny's well-paved streets, Carlow's fine ale and Bandon's staunch Protestants.[51]

As for the people, there were references to the kidnapping of heiresses,[52] and the widespread practice of duelling invariably featured, though Twiss, Young and Carr noted that it was in decline.[53] Bowden found his afternoon appointment cancelled after the gentleman in question was killed in a duel.[54] Clarke wrote of 'Duels without end', and Bush heard that even tradesmen were at it.[55] Derrick could see advantages in the casual violence that he saw in Cork, and lamented his inability to strike the insolent English lower orders without the threat of prosecution.[56] Addiction to gaming and swearing frequently cropped up.[57] As did excessive hospitality; more like ostentation remarked Bush, who had developed 'almost a disgust against every of their pretensions to it.'[58] Carr termed it 'barbarous conviviality'; 'frequently prejudicial to their fortunes' wrote George Cooper,[59] though others were more positive.[60] A notable feature of such a warm welcome was an encouragement to drink. Beware the treat of 'five times as much liquor poured down his throat as he would chuse', warned Bush, who condemned the practice. He found it 'superlatively contemptible', and betraying 'a sottish and grovelling taste'.[61]

Those looking for a pleasant place for this enforced drinking were out of luck. There were no London-style taverns, and inns were not usually of the requisite quality: 'not above two or three in the whole city that he could bear to be in', Bush proclaimed; others settled with 'dirty and ill-attended'.[62] Twiss felt that a traveller who was not 'over-nice' would be satisfied. Hotels were similar. Clarke referred to the 'exquisite filthiness' of 'Harris's hole' in Cope Street.[63] The famous Irish bulls usually made an appearance;[64] middlemen and absenteeism were condemned, and lack of specie bemoaned.[65] Most agreed with Campbell that indiscretions were uncommon among Irish women, but that did not save them from some rather impertinent comments.[66] Here Twiss was not the first, nor, as we shall see, the last, unchivalrous tourist. In his pre-Twiss – though unpublished – tour Burrows found that 'all the women here have high and broad foreheads, which in general gives them a disagreeable confident look'.[67] A later tourist said that Irish women were 'not very remarkable for beauty'.[68] In fact Burrows went beyond Twiss in a series of character-assassination vignettes, and it is difficult to see how his tour might have made it to print. Mrs Richard Mayne, wife of a yeoman farmer, was described as 'dirty beyond description', and Mrs Blayney's 'chilling drawl' was found wanting, as was her habit of winking at strangers.[69]

The lower orders rarely did even this well. They had 'no idea of English cleanliness', wrote Young.[70] 'A little attention in this particular would render them far less disgusting to others', commented a rival tourist,[71] and female aversion to stockings usually made an appearance.[72] Young claimed that lower-class women 'are as ugly as the women of fashion are handsome',[73] and similarly Campbell married the beauty of polite women with the 'indigent sloth' of their poorer counterparts.[74] The potato diet was commented on, occasionally in a positive manner; 'a corrective of the heat of the oaten diet', and 'propitious to fecundity' wrote Pococke and Carr respectively. Irish fondness for whiskey drinking astounded, and the number of dram shops in Dublin was estimated at 1,200 by Twiss, and increased to 12,000 by the miscopying Luckombe.[75] The typical Irish cabin's varied animal and human inhabitants usually cropped up, as did the 'abominable pile of filth' in front of it.[76] Both Bowden and Thomas Newenham compared it with the 'huts of savages'; Derrick found that 'the poorest hovel has its pigs and its cur-dogs', and Carr termed it a 'little antediluvian ark'.[77] One tourist went out of his way to praise the authenticity of Twiss's description of the 'beggarly cabins' in Dublin's suburbs, and, on their inhabitants, further mentioned 'the elegant amusement of clearing each other of vermin; all the different methods of performing which Mr Twiss seems to have observed with peculiar pleasure, as well as accuracy, in the course of his travels thro' Portugal and Ireland.'[78] Dubliners 'divesting each other of filth and vermin' also appeared in E.D. Clarke's tour.[79]

In this sense tours were as formulaic as romantic novels; the personal and individual only existed to order the descriptions, provide diversion and suggest truthfulness.[80] This meant they were ripe for satire and the English wit Edward Du Bois cashed in with *My pocket book; or, Hints for a 'ryghte merrie and conceitede' tour, in quarto to be called 'The stranger in Ireland' in 1805*, a jaunty take on Sir John Carr's tour, which could not help but satirize the genre as a whole. Twiss's tour was written according to 18th-century rules; and he was read, appreciated, and occasionally plagiarized, by his fraternity of fellow tourists. Nevertheless there were differences, usually predicated by the background of the tourists. Thomas Campbell's tour may have seemed a classic of the genre, but this Irish writer was actually using an accepted and popular mode to promote his country's needs to an English audience; Campbell's own distinctive Irish qualities were commented upon in Johnson's circle, including his being guilty of a 'bull'. Twiss's personality, purpose and inevitably his prose also had individual qualities. His supercilious attempts at humour were rarely matched elsewhere. For example, when observing Irish cabins he was able to distinguish them from pig-sties thanks to advertising boards. 'I was sure', he wrote, 'that hogs could not read'.[81] William Mavor's 1798 anthology of British tourism praised the 'judicious and liberal sentiments' of the likes of Topham Bowden and the Welshman Pennant, but saw Twiss's writings as akin to the 'great, but bigoted, JOHNSON'.[82] The fact that other tour writers commented on the severity of Twiss's work must also indicate that his barbs were sharper than those of his colleagues. Arthur Young playfully said that in his notes on Arbella Denny he would 'be as severe on her as ever Twiss was on her Country'.[83]

Subsequent tourists were as much a part of the anti-Twiss print assault as were Dublin's poets and hack writers. Many tourists made a deliberate effort to disprove Twiss's allegations; comments on his 'illiberality' abounded, though they often had a rather studied air.[84] Du Bois explained Carr's discourses on female stoutness of leg, partiality for port and forging of franks: 'Abuse the writer, and shew your gallantry.'[85] A tourist visiting in 1780 thought that 'there is more smartness than truth in Mr Twiss's observation upon the ladies legs'. He added that he 'should have confined his censure to females of inferior rank, the thickness of whose legs may be attributed partly to their wearing neither shoes nor stockings in their infancy, and partly to the far greater exercise they undergo than those whom fortune has exempted from labour.'[86] Thus he managed to exaggerate and reinforce Twiss's comments, plus reiterate another point – the stocking allergy – raised by the controversial writer. The name Twiss, in a very short period, had actually become a short-hand for shoddy tour-writing.

Others writers were more sympathetic. It was perhaps only natural that Elstob would prove a little defensive of Twiss, given that he had helped himself to sections of his tour. Elstob observed of the Irish: 'I am ashamed of them when I reflect on their behaviour to his effigy; – and their awkward sarcasms thrown out at that ingenious and worthy gentleman, show no good temper.' He confessed, however, that he was amused when confronted with a Twiss-pot. Elsewhere he found an Irishwoman who approved of the whole book, and thought it would produce good effects, except for one paragraph, that relating to female legs, although even here Elstob claimed that she was motivated by national partisanship to take up this subject.[87]

More bold visitors clearly sought to match Twiss in obnoxiousness; if they wanted to see for themselves, they also wished to sell for themselves. One tourist over in Ireland at the height of Free Trade and constitutional agitation, wrote that the 'only grievances that want redressing, arise chiefly from their own pride and laziness.' The food in the much-loved Eagle tavern 'furnished abundant exercise for our patience and our teeth'. A visit to a Catholic church led him to comment on 'the inexpressibly ridiculous fopperies of the priest, and the indecent filthiness of the place'. If this was not quite sufficient to have him christened as Twiss mark two then surely his chosen guide when he visited the Commons, the Castle supporting MP and ex-chief secretary Sir John

Blaquiere, would have done the trick.[88] In this case a press assault was hampered by the author's decision to levy his insults under the cloak of anonymity. E.D. Clarke was not so shy, and was happy to own up to his criticisms of Dublin in 1791: 'The streets are filled with wretchedness and grandeur, idleness and extravagance. It is not the habit of a few; it is the characteristic of the nation: A popular concern, to unite at once every species of dissipation, filthiness, and extortion.' At a Trinity College exhibition he noted that 'the women are always larger here than any body', and he thought the term 'DRAGGLE-TAILED SLUTS', peculiarly apposite for the many Dublin females who were ill-attired for the dirty streets.[89]

So why was there no Twiss-type response to these stern critics? Did Clarke get away with it because of the excitability of Dublin political-life in the early 1790s? The convulsions in France and their impact upon Ireland – the United Irishmen were formed in 1791, the year of his tour – were doubtless more interesting than the posturing of yet another querulous visitor. In any case, had not Twiss set an unbeatable standard? Rival claims to the title of piss-pot tourist were inadmissible. That others did not receive any response to their slurs can be explained by the all-consuming debate over union that occurred after the rebellion of 1798. Doubtless the very recent memory of pike-wielding peasants discouraged Protestants from leaping to the defence of Catholic Ireland.

Nevertheless, the potential still existed for a tour to inspire a satirical response. Sir John Carr was the unfortunate recipient, and his 1805 tour gave the public Edward Du Bois' spin-off, *My pocket book* lampooning his manner of collecting material. It was sufficiently popular to run into three editions. Carr was guilty of many of the same travel-guide sins as Twiss. He was anecdotal, keen to generalize based on the flimsiest evidence and eager to place Ireland at a disadvantage in comparison with other European sites. His tour was also replete with quotations from other works, though at an eighth of the book's length he could not hope to match the scissor-happy Richard Twiss. While not quite cutting and pasting, he was prepared to rehash anecdotes – even one fictional, from Maria Edgeworth – as his own.[90] Many of these were as churlish and ignorant as those of Twiss. Carr was following Twiss in aiming to entertain, and to sell, hence his six volumes of tours between 1803 and 1811. And like Twiss he was less than keen on some ribbing from the press, ultimately failing in the legal action he took out against the booksellers responsible for the spoof tour.[91]

3. Publication and popular reaction

Following the publication of *A tour in Ireland*, Irish patriot newspapers rushed to defend their country and their most impoverished region. Some of Twiss's comments were exaggerated, others invented, and aspersions were cast on his character. Dublin's *Freeman's Journal* and *Hibernian Journal* took the lead in this campaign, with able support from an army of hack writers, whose work was either published, or at least advertised, in these newspapers. Contributions were varied, though there was certainly unity of purpose. The *Londonderry Journal* and the *Hibernian Chronicle* did their readers the service of gutting the book for its most poisonous extracts. The *Londonderry Journal* quoted Twiss on the indigence of the middle classes, his sense of 'intellectual retrogradation', the 'mediocrity of knowledge, between learning and ignorance', the forging of franks and, of course, the uncommon thickness of female legs.[1]

The *Hibernian Journal* serialized the anonymous Dublin-focused *Letters on the Irish nation*, written by an Englishmen to a friend in London, as an antidote to Twiss's *Tour*. In this sense it was a publishing war. The author made it clear that he was battling against an English readership and a putative French translation, and that he had chosen the *Hibernian Journal* because it was read in London.[2] The introduction to this series – also puffed in *Faulkner's Dublin Journal* and the *Londonderry Journal* – was published in the 21–23 August issue, and the *Hibernian Journal* went on to publish 13 letters. However, after discourses upon religious matters, Irish architecture and literature, the framing of parliamentary bills and the aldermanic system of representation the editors appeared to realize that though a very worthy response to Twiss, the author was actually displaying a little too much candour; the Irish Parliament being described as having 'a Mean Appearance'; the Tholsel, 'a large heavy Stone Building, in which is seen neither Taste nor Elegance', and 'a total Disregard of Uniformity' spoiling the beauty of St Stephen's Green. Perhaps more importantly the *Letters on the Irish nation* were also deathly dull, and they were quickly replaced by the Twiss-inspired comedic series 'Cornelius O'Dowde's *Tour through Dublin*'.[3] Thanks to the cut-and-paste approach, plenty of fictive tours had been published. But O'Dowde's tour had more in common with the picaresque romps beloved of Tobias Smollett. O'Dowde, a down-to-earth Connacht man, began: 'Tour Writing is the Fashion – and why should myself be out of the Fashion.'[4]

Both the *Freeman's Journal* and the *Hibernian Journal* promoted *A defence of Ireland: a poem* by Richard Lewis, a writer who proclaimed his patriotic credentials by dedicating the piece to the radical MP, Sir Edward Newenham, and by praising Thomas Paine in a footnote.[5] The *Freeman's Journal* published poetry in praise of Lewis, 'Whose satire can sink to confusion and shame, The snakes who his country betray or defame'.[6] A fictional Lewis contributed to the footnotes in – and added patriotic integrity to – another anti-Twiss work, *An answer to a poetical epistle from Madam Teresa Pinna Ÿ Ruiz*.[7] This latter piece by the lawyer Leonard MacNally marked a high-point in the incestuous outpouring of satirical works, as it was written in response, not to Twiss, but to William Preston's *An heroic epistle from Donna Teresa Pinna* and *An heroic answer, from Richard Twiss*. These two works by the Irish poet and playwright were the most influential, and certainly the most widely cited in the Irish and English press, of the anti-Twiss propaganda pieces. The first of these mocked Twiss's gallantry whilst in Spain, and the second humorously tackled his Irish allegations, turning some of them against the tourist, before reflecting upon the anti-Twiss reaction.[8] The *Hibernian Journal* published a sonnet lauding Preston, the author happy to celebrate 'Satire's keenest Darts', whether the butt was Twiss or Preston's earlier target, the famous provost of Trinity College and place-hunter, John Hely-Hutchinson.[9]

There is a sense that Twiss and Dublin's patriot poets and printers were involved in a very knowing cycle of self-promotion; all eager to bolster their careers by latching onto the latest cause célèbre. Twiss, it seems, knew the Dublin-born Preston, and had come across his work in the anti-Hely-Hutchinson *Pranceriana* whilst in Dublin.[10] Preston was at the Middle Temple in London in the mid-1770s and he may have read the Irish tour before its publication in Ireland, perhaps even discussing it with Twiss. Preston had obviously made him aware of his plan to write a poetical response. Twiss commented: 'The little jew poet told me lately he intended to write a Heroic Epistle to me, I told him he was very welcome if he thought it might bring him into notice.'[11] *An heroic epistle from Donna Teresa Pinna* was one of the first anti-Twiss publications, and it is difficult to determine whether it was begun before or after the publication of *A tour in Ireland*. The direct references to the tour are few in number and rather bland; namely the delights of St Stephen's Green and the use of noddies, two wheel horse-drawn chaises. Twiss's plan to compile a 'muster-roll' of Irish beauties, which so threatened Donna Teresa Pinna, his would-be Spanish amour, did not make it to the page.[12] How then can we explain these references? It is possible that Preston had seen snippets of text, or had conversations with Twiss on the book's content; otherwise he was showing remarkable restraint in keeping his powder dry.

If the former then Preston must have based this poem on expectation built up by the tone of the Spanish tour, along with his own impressions of Twiss. Dublin's hacks were ready for him and he may have been undone by the close connections between the Grantham circle in Spain and some influential Irish politicians. Robinson had not warmed to Twiss as time passed in Spain: 'Mr Twiss is still here', he rather resignedly observed, and 'he has not yet given us any reason to alter our opinions of him, or to make wish him to delay his departure.'[13] Grantham agreed with his brother, commenting on Twiss's vulgarity, which initially appeared somewhat entertaining: 'He will probably dine here. Our young gentlemen think him a great Treat. Perhaps he will be shy before us.' This feeling, for Grantham at least, quickly passed: 'Mr Twiss has taken his leave of us which I am very glad of, for I always thought myself likely to have trouble on his account – as he is so forward, so ignorant, & so fond designedly of getting into scrapes.'[14] Most prominent among these Irish friends of the Grantham circle was Francis Andrews, bon viveur and provost of Trinity College Dublin before Hely-Hutchinson. He was a friend of Grantham and Robinson and had been staying with Grantham whilst Twiss was in Spain. Lord Shelburne, a regular visitor to Dublin and his estates in Ireland in the early 1770s, was a good friend of Frederick Robinson,[15] and Shelburne had his own entry into Dublin's print world through Sir James Caldwell and Faulkner. Other correspondents of the Spanish diplomatic circle included the absentee Irish peer Lord Fitzwilliam, and the owner of Dublin's baths, Dr Achmet.

Notwithstanding Samuel Johnson's lazy praise it is clear that the Spanish tour did not go down well in all quarters. Frederick Robinson was led to believe that his book 'is a very poor performance'.[16] Even so, Twiss's sales of his Spanish tour were good, and he was therefore dismissive of any response to his Irish trip, and doubtless hoped a scrap would help him to sell a few more copies. He was certainly scornful of the talents of the Dublin hacks. Discussing one, possibly Richard Lewis, he found 'nothing novel' in his rhymes, observing that 'they may be applied in the same manner and almost in the same sense as children's copies, such as "A Man of Deeds & not of words, is like a garden full of Turds"'. He continued: 'I do not doubt the inclination of the poet to be satirical if he could, but the woeful lack of abilities prevents him.' And then rather pompously added: 'as to any attack upon *me* he might as well attempt to overset the pyramid of Egypt with a squirt.'[17]

Twiss obviously saw himself as part of a far superior literary sphere, yet these turds and squirts would come back to haunt him. Yes, controversy was good for sales, but he must surely have been taken aback by the violence of the Irish response, and its ability to embrace a broad section of society. This was partly because Twiss's book arrived at a moment when the patriotic-print nexus was simmering nicely. Booksellers were becoming more organized, and the Society of Dublin Booksellers was formed in the year that his tour was published. Other key figures in Dublin print took leading roles, including Michael Mills at the *Hibernian Journal* and Samuel Leathley at the *Freeman's Journal*; the latter allowed anti-Twiss poetry to dominate the newspaper's Parnassiad column for well over six months. George Faulkner appeared in several pieces – thanks to his appearance in the tour – and was lavished with praise by Richard Lewis and others.[18] Twiss's fake gallows speech was addressed to his successor at *Faulkner's Dublin Journal*, Thomas Todd Faulkner. Outside of Dublin, John Ferrar, printer of the *Limerick Chronicle*, personally wrote a lengthy response that also reached the Cork and Kilkenny press.[19] William Flyn's *Hibernian Chronicle* did a remarkable hatchet job on the tour, cataloguing all of the best Twiss-isms in two columns for his Cork readership. Finally, Thomas Walker of *Walker's Hibernian Magazine* published a caricature of Twiss, which was sold by booksellers in Belfast and Newry.[20]

The gallows speech addressed to Thomas Todd Faulkner suggested that one of the tourist's more serious crimes was 'the horrid practice of writing nonsense and abusing the press'.[21] It was appropriate then that the press took its revenge, and newspaper readers would have delighted in seeing Twiss crop up in every aspect of the newspaper's design, including obituaries, letters to the editor, even a 'card' inserted by Twiss offering his services to young gentlemen wishing for an escort on the Grand Tour.[22] In fact Twiss allowed Dublin's printers and satirists to demonstrate the sophistication of their art-form, as is shown in the blurring between fact and fiction and the constant self-referencing. Dublin political quarrels dominated MacNally's *An Answer to a poetical epistle*. This fake response by Twiss to Teresa Pinna Ÿ Ruiz was used to make numerous jibes at individuals in the political and literary spheres. The lawyer Richard Sheridan was mocked for his want of a university education; Dr Patrick Duignan, Trinity College intriguer, and later Protestant Ultra was treated with peculiar scorn, and Samuel Whyte, who ran an Academy in Grafton Street and wrote his own lofty anti-Twiss poem despite being praised in the tour, was a repeat target, frequently ribbed for his linguistic pedantry. We also find the vital cogs of Dublin print culture chipping in with irrelevancies, including a hairdresser and his puffing advertisements in the *Hibernian Journal*; hopeful civic politicians promising to regulate prostitution, and apothecaries hawking cures for measled pigs. In this sense perhaps it is best to show caution before evaluating attitudes to Twiss's tour in terms of an English–Irish clash: this was a very local dispute.[23]

Indeed it is clear that many from the local print world were profiting from Twiss's work in a way that by-passed patriotism. The fact that authors did not have copyright in Ireland allowed publishers to take unfettered advantage of any London-published sensation. Exshaw printed uncontroversial snippets from the descriptions of Lough Erne, Ballyshannon and the Giant's Causeway.[24] Edmond Finn in Kilkenny secured copies of *Travels through Portugal and Spain* as did the Dame Street bookseller James Potts; although here there was earlier interest in marketing tours as he had also published Bush's *Hibernia curiosa*.[25] John Ferrar, despite his personal intervention against Twiss, was happy to publish the light-fingered Elstob's apology for the tourist.[26] Twiss's *A trip to Paris, in July and August, 1792* had its own separate Dublin publication in 1793. In Belfast James Magee had his shop well-stocked with copies of *A tour in Ireland*, and of course plenty of newspapers carried advertisements for booksellers stocking the tour, including *Faulkner's Dublin Journal* and *Saunders News-Letter*.[27]

Booksellers and newspaper printers obviously benefited from the rumpus, along with Twiss. But so did the likes of Lewis and Preston. The advertisement for Lewis's *Seventeen hundred and seventy-seven; or, A picture of the manners and character of the age* made it clear that it was 'By the author of an Heroic Epistle to Richard Twiss Esq'. Lewis also quoted at length from his *Defence of Ireland* in his *Dublin Guide*, published twelve years later.[28] The author of 'Letters on the Irish Nation' selflessly proclaimed his willingness to have them reprinted together 'in another Form and Size'.[29] Preston's work resonated in Britain long after the 1770s. The bookseller James Lackington included a quotation from *An heroic epistle* in his memoirs, and just as Twiss's tour was remembered by David Rivers in his *Literary memoirs*, so were Preston's 'two elegant and spirited poetical satires'.[30]

Although the anti-Twiss backlash was much fomented by Dublin's publishers, it eventually became more than a print war. Even the upper echelons of polite Irish society were drawn into the fray. A masquerade party at the house of the banker David LaTouche, attended 'by some of the principal Nobility', was marked by the public recitation of one of the less vulgar anti-Twiss poems, written by Samuel Whyte, a figure in a patriotic amateur dramatic circle that included Henry Grattan and Walter Hussey Burgh. Subscribers to Whyte's *Poems on various subjects* of 1792 would include John Philpott Curran, Lord Edward Fitzgerald, Leonard MacNally and William Preston.[31] LaTouche was not the only city politician involved in the fray, as a Dublin alderman had apparently stood for the portrait designed to be emblazoned within the chamber pot. Over in Trinity College, students joined in the poetical attack with gusto.[32] And the correspondence of the MPs James Fortescue and Owen Wynne, who sat for a Connacht constituency, reveals that they were of a similar mind.[33] The New Theatre at Fishamble Street performed the anti-Twiss play *A trip to Ireland; or, The tour-writer* on two occasions; with the actor and manager John Vandermere reading the prologue. The first performance provoked 'uncommon Peals of Laughter and Applause, insomuch that it was almost impossible, at several Times, to hear the Performers.'[34] Elsewhere Richard and Maria Edgeworth recounted a conversation in which it was alleged – unfairly according to Twiss – that he had made the assertion that 'if you look at an Irish lady, she answers, "port if you please"'.[35] As with many of the anti-Twiss barbs, the truth behind it mattered not, and it quickly entered the canon of Twiss-isms. Similarly John Carr made a point of ridiculing the charge that Irish women were 'naturally bacchanalian', even though it had not appeared in Twiss's tour.[36]

Twiss may have been condescending about his poetical assassins, but, as we shall see, he could not be quite so blasé about hostile responses from other sections of the Irish community. The Irish press was far reaching, and its population willing to travel. The Irish were involved in a riot in Bath in 1769, in support of their favoured successor to Samuel Derrick as master of ceremonies,[37] and the anti-Twiss response in newspaper columns, if not published stanzas, promised violent retribution. The rumoured beating suffered by Twiss at the hands of a Connacht man described below, if true, must in part be put down to the willingness of Irish newspapers to keep returning to this particular story in news articles, letters, squibs and various satirical pieces. The Irish press misled their readers by asserting that Twiss's name had been struck from the Royal Society, 'as a disgrace to literature'.[38] According to a fanciful piece in the *Hibernian Journal* he had 'above TWENTY TIMES, in the course of three Months' suffered the indignity of being 'kicked out of Company, slapped in the Face, and Horse-whipped'.[39]

Newspapers also created more imaginative slurs on the nation, and some of these were rather convincing; a letter from Twiss to a friend in Cambridge, purloined by a *Hibernian Journal* correspondent, being close enough to Twiss's original comments to invest them with a ring of truth. 'I find the Men', a fictitious Twiss wrote, 'ignorant, clownish, and without a Glimmering of what is called refined Life'. 'The women here', he continued, 'are the most awkward, horrid, ugly Devils you ever saw', and even the prettiest 'have legs as thick as the Irish Chairmen in Covent Garden', with 'Hands, Arms and Breasts … as red as Blood Puddings'. He added: 'I have not seen among all their toasted Beauties one Woman with whom a Man of Sentiment or Taste could pass twelve Hours without being nauseated.'[40] Though this was a print culture that was immersed in satire it is certainly possible that some of the more credible pieces were not regarded as fictive.

Newspapers also encouraged the use of Twiss's name in contexts other than travel writing or chamber pots. *Finn's Leinster Journal* reported on a quarrel in a Dublin printers which saw one workman fling 'a font of types' at a fellow for proposing that rather than be termed 'a Devil' by his workmates he should in future be called 'a Twiss'.[41] The *Hibernian Journal* claimed that the phrase: 'He is as great a Liar as TWISS' was in common usage, as was the word Twiss as a synonym for an untruth.[42] Twiss apparently became known as 'lying Dick'.[43]

The success of the propaganda war against Twiss was demonstrated by the fact that anti-Twiss sentiment appeared to take hold amongst the lower orders, very possibly uniting Protestant and Catholic. A correspondent of the *Belfast News-Letter* claimed that 'the vulgar, always listening to the conversation of their superiors, heard of the publication, and it incensed them', and that if he had been in Ireland 'they would have handled the author of it a little roughly'.

His name was 'dirt' – in the Swiftian sense of the word – in the privies of Dublin's House of Industry.[44] The ubiquitous chamber pots might have served Twiss well, as one commentator credited the entrepreneurial potter with 'calming the minds of the people'. He observed: 'The meanest of the people are pleased – and they think themselves amply revenged, when nature calls, to p-ss upon their calumniator.'[45]

In August 1776 the *Hibernian Journal, Finn's Leinster Journal* and *Londonderry Journal* all reported that a party of chimney sweeps in Ennis, Co. Clare had processed to Gallows Green with a copy of Twiss's *A tour in Ireland.* They smeared it with soot, and then had it burned by the Common hangman before hundreds of spectators.[46] Kevin Whelan cites this incident as evidence of a 'nationalist turn' that paved the way for the 1798 rebellion. However in his quotation from the version carried by *Finn's Leinster Journal* he does not include reference to the initial planning meeting, which took place 'at the king of Morocco's head in Sooty-lane'.[47] It is possible that this tale, like many others involving Twiss, was fictional. But this rather sophisticated variant of popular protest was not uncommon amongst Ireland's artisans during this period. Many of the protests that took place in Dublin's liberties were ritualistic, and involved some sort of parade, which would gather spectators along the way, and then culminate in some sort of mock execution. In August 1776 journeymen weavers planned to parade through Dublin with a hearse, on top of which they would put 'a piece of coarse scarlet cloth, covered with a black crape, as an emblem of the present situation of our woollen manufacture.' Apparently they had even gone as far as to hire female keeners from Co. Kerry.[48]

A fictional chimney sweep club should not lead us to discount the notion of the further radicalization of Irish patriotism during the Twiss backlash. After all, these articles were appearing alongside news and commentary on the American War of Independence. Approval of the Wilkite cause was given in 'Letters on the Irish nation', the author celebrating the freedom to report parliamentary debates in Ireland, in comparison with England. The same writer attacked the use of Poynings' Law in the Irish legislative system, and English absentees holding offices in the Irish legal system.[49] Twiss's two most prominent protagonists, Richard Lewis and William Preston were both intimately caught up in Dublin's patriotic civic life. Preston was linked to the most senior patriot peer Lord Charlemont and would join him as a member of the patriotic club the Monks of Screw, and later write for the United Irish newspaper the *Press.* Preston's anti-Twiss poems were published in the same year as his satire on the British evacuation from Boston.[50] Lewis was made an honorary member of the radical Dublin Legion Volunteers, and the praise for Newenham and Paine in Lewis's *A defence of Ireland* has already been mentioned. It is also worth noting that Leonard MacNally would become a United Irishman, act as legal counsel for Napper Tandy and write verse for the *Northern Star.*

Given this line-up the impact of the political views of tourists should not be underestimated. Samuel Derrick's admiration for John Wilkes doubtless went down well with some Irishmen.[51] After Twiss, tours became a way of demonstrating patriot sympathies. Campbell, Bush and the author of *A general history of Ireland* published in 1781 all expressed support for commercial relief, and the Revd William Hamilton dedicated his trip to Antrim to Charlemont.[52] It was difficult for tourists not to become embroiled in Irish political controversies, or if we take a more cynical view, have an eye on patriotic sales post-Twiss. A tourist visiting in 1780 was none too impressed with the Volunteers, referring to 'a military rage, or puerile fondness for the insignia of Mars'. He warned of the dangers of turning self-important notions against their mother country.[53] But it was much more likely that tourists would sympathize with patriotic concerns and a number of writers advocated a shift in Ireland's status from colony to commercial partner. At the same time in the great debates that shaped Protestant Ascendancy, tourists were critical of the ruling oligarchy and landlord oppression. In stark contrast, Twiss had been keen to advise tough measures against rural protestors, and when this was referred to in a 1798 abridgement of his work, he happily took the credit for a policy which if enacted would apparently have prevented the rebellion of that year.[54]

Twiss's connections with Townshend's print men Caldwell, Gorges Edmond Howard, a Dublin Castle hack and playwright much derided in the press, and even Faulkner, gave his tour a clear political slant, and they enabled satirists to link Twiss with unpopular Castle supporters like John Hely-Hutchinson and Sir John Blaquiere. An epistle written to Twiss by Timothy Mendax reminds the reader not only of Ben Johnson's fabricating tourist from *The Sad Shepherd*, but also of a character in the anti-Hely-Hutchinson volume, *Pranceriana*.[55] Preston had contributed to this work and the original satires were carried in the *Hibernian Journal*. Indeed its printer Michael Mills was kidnapped and roughed up by outraged Trinity College students. Mills used Twiss in the continued campaign against Hely-Hutchinson, and his newspaper had the tourist defend the provost's reforms to the Trinity College curriculum as 'the only polite Improvement the City can boast'.[56] Hely-Hutchinson's chief opponent in the Trinity College squabble, Patrick Duigenan, also linked the two men in one of his anti-Hely-Hutchinson pamphlets. He described the provost's written style as 'inferior to that of Twiss' and in a footnote reminded his readers that the latter was 'an illiterate buffoon'.[57] In MacNally's *An answer to a poetical epistle* Blaquiere was compared to a 'gallows culprit', and the Castle government was criticized for having 'turned out a Man who served them faithfully for twenty years' in order to secure the new chief secretary the Co. Dublin seat. One of the many commentaries added to *An answer to a poetical epistle*, had a McD-rm-t, in response to Twiss's jibes about filthy gutters, boast: 'Ld T-wns-nd allowed no Man could do a dirty Job, cleaner than I could.' In the *Hibernian Journal* a fictionalized Gorges Howard was willing to deal with enquiries relating to Twiss's Grand Tour escort advertisement.[58]

The strand of this patriotic attack dealing with Dublin politics merits further investigation. It is clear that some writers favoured a scattergun approach, assailing radicals and Castle-men alike. In *An answer to a poetical epistle* Leonard MacNally lampooned Richard Sheridan's Free Citizens-funded legal defence of Michael Mills, following his pasting by Trinity College students.[59] Twiss, the poem's hero, commented directly on the Free Citizens:

> If at the Court my Measures chance to fail,
> I'll turn free Citizen, and learn to rail:
> Drink Treason, Adams, Handcock, Lee, Montgomery
> That valiant Man, of most immortal Memory.
> Not our Knight President [Sir Edward Newenham] shall louder roar,
> Then I'll get drunk, reel Home to Bed, and snore.

Obviously any sniping from the mouth of Twiss would only have elevated the character of the Free Citizens. But the views of MacNally, through a commentary by 'Richard Sheridan', reveal that the anti-Twiss writers were far from united on Dublin's radical political culture. The Free Citizens, 'Sheridan' helpfully explained, were 'A very respectable Body, who became Free, by being Slaves to the Will of the Majority'. He offered the post of the society's toast-maker to 'he who gives most Treason, and commits *old Riot the newest kind of way*'; a reflection on the lengthy lists of toasts regularly published in the *Hibernian Journal*. Doubtless Richard Lewis as a friend of Sir Edward Newenham would have raised an eyebrow at the reference to the President 'Dapper Ned'. And Lewis himself was given some gentle ribbing, 'because I advertised that I would write Petitions and addresses for any Patriot whatsoever; but that I would never write for a Place-Man, or pensioner'; the barb here being that he was providing his services for the 'OUTS', those who wanted places and pensions.[60]

It is clear therefore that the patriotic church – as defined by the anti-Twiss coalition – was both broad and incestuous. There was no 'national turn' as such; patriotism was much too complex a credo to be seen in that kind of light. For example, the author of the *Hibernian Journal's* 'Letters on the Irish nation' took Hely-Hutchinson's part in the Trinity College ruckus and in 1784 the Castle-supporting *Volunteer Evening Post* took the same anti-Twiss stance as its earlier radical counterparts. In the 1790s William Preston revealed his misgivings about the French revolution in his play *Democratic Rage*, and, famously, Leonard MacNally turned informer against his United Irish colleagues.[61]

Also worth bearing in mind is that while sympathy was shown to maligned Catholic fellow citizens in many of the anti-Twiss pieces, Protestant punsters could not quite rid themselves of old-whig attitudes. Thus despite the tourist's rare praise for the obelisk at the Boyne, a determined attempt was made to tarnish Twiss's reputation by alleging that he had connections with a faith that was antipathetic to liberty. In his fake gallows speech Twiss admitted that he had converted to Catholicism to atone for debauching the daughter of Donna Teresa Ruiz, and that he died 'an unworthy member of the Church of Rome'.[62] That other soft-target for the *Hibernian Journal* hacks, John Hely-Hutchinson, was attacked for his role in 'EXTENDING the further Growth of POPERY through this kingdom.' Even Cornelius O'Dowde took time out from his fashionable diversions to refer to William, 'our great Deliverer', in a speech lambasting the inclusion of a statue of James II on the Tholsel.[63] It must be stressed then that this was a very particular point in patriotic development. Old whig values were extremely important to the likes of Sir Edward Newenham and the Free Citizens of Dublin, and the superficial unity of the anti-Twiss reaction actually contained two strains of Protestant thought; one of which was fundamentally opposed to the full admission of Catholics into the Irish polity.

Indeed if one is searching for post-Twiss optimism on the religious question, then tourists were a better bet than many Dublin radicals. Campbell, though no great fan of Gaelic Ireland, opposed the Penal Laws and Arthur Young described them as 'the marks of illiberal barbarism'. Another tourist was surprised by the degree of respect shown to William III, which was 'little short of adoration'.[64] Bowden may have visited an Orange Lodge in Belfast, but any sympathy that he might have had for its brethren was couched in opposition to government electoral corruption. Post union, John Carr described the fourth of November festivities in Dublin as an 'offensive ceremony'.[65]

4. Twiss and Irish cultural life

The Irish press was particularly exercised by Twiss's charges against Ireland of cultural and commercial deficiencies, partly because these were directed at the Ascendancy, and partly because there was more than a veneer of truth in them. It seems that Irish commentators were unaware of the unofficial rules of the tour of Ireland. Visitors arrived expecting little that was worthy of praise in the urban environment; though Dublin's dirty streets and Cork's bloody ones were noteworthy. Therefore on these points Twiss was not markedly out of step with other tourists. His remark that neither of the Dublin cathedrals 'are remarkable for their architecture' was similar to Campbell's assessment of these 'mean Gothic buildings'.[1]

Yet Twiss's attacks were somehow more personal, certainly more pointed, and rarely leavened with praise. In fact from the late 1740s tourists had begun to highlight pockets of urban improvement, and praise was lavished on the architectural advances seen in Dublin during the 1770s and 1780s. Arthur Young, in Dublin only a year after Twiss, wrote that 'the public buildings are magnificent'.[2] Burrows remarked that St Stephen's Green was 'much more pleasant, and quite as spacious, and well built as any square in London'. A tour in 1780 described the Exchange as 'a very magnificent and elegant building'. A year later the Hibernian School in Phoenix Park was termed 'a large and magnificent stone building'.[3] Merrion Square was 'built in a superb style', and there was praise from Bowden for the Custom House.[4] The two plagiarists-in-chief, Elstob and Luckombe, were very fond of the Lying-In Hospital and Bush praised Trinity College library.[5]

Urban development was, therefore, one area on which Twiss was largely out of step with other tourists. Outside of the capital city Chetwood referred to Cork's 'magnificent Buildings' and Holmes liked its 'handsome custom-house and exchange'. A later tourist sniffed at Twiss's failure to recognize the statue of Chatham in the mayoralty house.[6] In 1752 Pococke regarded Limerick as 'a very dirty disagreeable place', but Bowden, Holmes and Carr praised Limerick new town, with its handsome streets and elegant shops.[7] Bush claimed that Derry was 'the cleanest, best built, and most beautifully situated of any town in Ireland', and Kilkenny, noted for its politeness and civility, was compared to Oxford.[8] The tourist most impressed with Ireland's provincial towns, Bowden, described Cashel as a handsome town that was 'remarkable for the finest and most perfect remains of Gothic architecture'; struggling for adjectives he also used 'handsome' to describe Strabane, Derry, Coleraine and Drogheda.[9]

The bedrock of Peter Borsay's English urban renaissance was the leisure town.[10] Much-visited Killarney needed improvement according to Twiss and Young, in terms of both amusements and accommodation. Mallow, Ireland's premier spa town, in Twiss's opinion, fell short of the standards set by English resorts. Ever ready to find fault, he noted: 'Mallow is termed by the natives the Irish Bath; but an Englishman would rather, from the meanness of the accommodations, deem it an apology for a watering-place.'[11] Campbell offered support, referring to Mallow's 'tepid spring', which was in the process of being abandoned by its devotees in favour of Bristol, 'where if the waters are not better, it must be allowed that the accommodations are.'[12] Others were keen to challenge Twiss's description, and Bowden termed it a 'neat little town and most happily circumstanced'.[13] Some towns fared better in the eyes of tourists. In Blackrock Carr found 'a taste in building displayed, which is rarely exhibited in England'. The small spa town of Castle-connell had 'numerous genteel lodging-houses', a good inn, and an elegant season.[14] Time constraints meant that Twiss was unable to see all of these sights. John Ferrar complained that Twiss's post-haste style of journey had deprived him of some of Ireland's gems, such as Thomastown, 'where hospitality, elegance, nature, art, exotics and domestics combine to render it a most delightful place'.[15]

When discussing Dublin's leisure opportunities, Twiss was typically terse and ungenerous, restricting his comments to the balls at the Castle, the peculiar decor of Smock Alley, and concerts held elsewhere in the city. Notice of those at the Lying-In Hospital was accompanied by what appeared to be one of several barbs directed at Irish fecundity. He also compared Ranelagh gardens to London's White Conduit house and Bagnigge-wells. This may not have been a deliberate slight, but only two years later Fanny Burney would poke fun at these two very middle-class entertainment venues.[16] In contrast, though not feeling spoiled by the available diversions, the usually acerbic Burrows likened the Rotunda and its gardens adjoining the Lying-In Hospital to London's Ranelagh and he enjoyed the ride through Phoenix Park.[17]

Indeed for the most part tourists had plenty of positive thoughts on the burgeoning leisure opportunities, and, in its broadest sense, the public sphere, and the likes of Derrick, master of ceremonies at Bath and Tunbridge Wells, and Parker, a public lecturer, were experts in this area. Arthur Young bulled up the good society in Dublin. He talked of the two 'very well regulated' gentleman's clubs, Anthry's and Daly's, and of assemblies at Fishamble Street and the Rotunda.[18] Campbell said that according to female testimony, 'the social pleasures are more easily obtained here than in London'.[19] Carr noted the new club-house that housed Daly's on College Green, described by Bowden as 'the most superb gambling house'.[20] As for theatres, 'one of the most elegant and best constructed' could be found in Smock Alley, and playhouses in Crow Street and Aungier Street also had their fans.[21] Campbell and – inevitably – Luckombe were less impressed with Dublin's coffee-houses, finding them few in number, used only for tea and coffee, and not for dinner and supper, as in London. Bush signed off his tour from Lucas's Coffee-House. Bowden was positive about Dublin's societies and charities.[22] Carr was disappointed to find 'such a paucity of literary societies, and of periodical literary publications' in Dublin, but he did include a sizeable section on the charitable societies and institutions in Cork. Indeed the theatres, coffee-houses and assembly rooms of provincial Ireland seemed to offer reasonably diverting fare.[23]

The likes of Carr and Newenham were touring Ireland after three decades of extensive urban development that would transform Dublin. Yet much had already been achieved by 1775, and given the reliance upon the cut-and-paste approach, it is clear that tourists felt that conveying a sense of linear progression in the urban world was unimportant. In 1773 Burrows had denied that there was any class between upper and lower, and bemoaned the 'small choice of the little elegancies of life' in Dublin shops. But unlike Twiss, who listed in mundane detail the goods sold by petty shopkeepers, Burrows had no need to be sensitive to an audience.[24] In contrast Elstob was impressed by female book-keeping and Campbell-Luckombe praised the urbanity of the merchant class.[25] So Twiss once again appeared churlish when he noted the indigence of Dublin's middle-classes, finding that 'there are many shops, which serve at once for two different trades; such as silversmiths and booksellers; saddlers and milliners'. He also criticized the nature of shop and street signs, hence the slight in Twiss's fictional letter to Cambridge designed to rile the combustible Liberty Boys; a pub sign in their demesne depicted 'a large Green Lion with these Words under it *this is the Sign of the Golden Fleece.*'[26]

Twiss's attack on Dublin urban and commercial life was felt very keenly. After all this was the world in which printers and writers lived. They had perhaps become inured to the usual derogatory comments directed at the rural peasantry and the praise offered to the surrounding landscape. Yet Burrows' unpublished tour hinted at future Twiss-isms: 'I hear but of one literary man of eminence in the country, who is Dr Leland', and later: 'They print wretchedly, and though it is cheaper than ours, yet it is so bad that a man who loves his money would rather buy our books.'[27] Lack of regulation in the Irish print trade might suggest that he had a point, but print men were influential individuals, and newspapers sophisticated organs. Thus when Twiss attacked the press itself, claiming printers used cheap brown paper and that Irish newspapers were 'curiosities, by reason of their style and spelling,' he was engaging with a punchy and well-marshalled force. That Richard Lewis took the pseudonym 'corrector of the press' is telling, and a response to Twiss's claim that there were none.[28]

Twiss had complained that 'every printer in the island is at liberty to print, and every bookseller to vend as many, and as vile editions of any book, as they please'.[29] His views chimed with those of Catholic antiquarian Charles O'Conor, who, writing to George Faulkner on the subject of intellectual property rights, went further, observing: 'In other Countries the press is *restrained*, from doing Good; In Ireland it is *permitted* to do acknowledged Evil, even to the Public as well as to Individuals.'[30] Predecessors had been eager to praise Irish newspapers and their proprietors. After all it was often their print shops that would stock their tours. *Faulkner's Dublin Journal* was lauded over English rivals by Chetwood, who also mentioned the *Cork Journal* and admired that town's bookshops.[31] Even Elstob departed from Twiss when it came to describing Dublin's printers at work, finding an example with 'tolerable good paper, and with a pretty neat type'. He also asserted that a corrector was in attendance.[32] Bowden's eulogy owed much to his brother's involvement in the London newspaper business. He noted that newspapers in Ireland 'are spirited and well supported' and that it 'was the press which diffused the spirit of volunteering throughout the kingdom.' He added: 'No writings are admired in the newspapers which are not highly seasoned with patriotism and reflections on government.'[33]

In terms of cultural achievements Twiss reserved his most scabrous commentary for Irish art and architecture, though originally he had included a jibe at the Irish playwright Gorges Howard, criticizing him, somewhat hypocritically, for his self-regarding tone.[34] After coming to know the man in Dublin, he excised these pages from his book. Yet it was true that Howard's talents were limited, and he was tainted by his reputation as a Castle hack and pamphleteer during the Money Bill dispute; Robert Jephson had already produced a bitingly satirical exchange of verse between Howard and the publisher George Faulkner, much enjoyed by Twiss, and coincidentally used by the Edgeworths to lampoon John Carr.[35] However by 1776 Faulkner was being feted as the father of the Irish newspaper – 'courteous Faulkner, with his honest mind'[36] – and opinions were divided on Jephson; after viewing one of his operas an *Hibernian Journal* contributor claimed that he wrote 'Without the Aid of Art, in Nature's Spite'.[37] But this was still a close call. The press was much more decided on the ridiculous Howard, and Twiss may have missed an opportunity to distance himself from the Castle hacks. One patriot scribbler clearly thought that Howard was indebted to Twiss, as he mischievously claimed that the writer was acting as his intermediary, taking enquiries from gentry and noble families wishing Twiss to accompany a son on the Grand Tour.[38]

Perhaps Twiss's most damning indictment of Irish culture came in his attack on the fine arts, and this again reveals something about the Ascendancy mind in the latter 18th century, and is thus worth examining in a little more detail. Twiss commented: 'In regard to the fine arts, Ireland is yet considerably behind-hand with the rest of Europe, partly owing to the unsettled state in which that island was, during civil wars and commotions'. He complained that 'out of Dublin, and its environs, there is scarcely a single capital picture, statue, or building, to be found in the whole island.'[39] Twiss, of course, did not have the recommendations that would have been required to see private treasures, and as with many tourists there is more detail on the gardens of the great houses. Thus we do not have the encomiums on houses like Powerscourt and Castletown, 'the most superb private house in his Majesty's dominions' wrote Bowden.[40] But if we ignore Twiss's patronizing tone, his comment was essentially the same as Burrows' conviction, in 1773, that 'there are few or no pieces of the fine arts in this kingdom, either made by the natives or imported from foreign countries.' Other visitors were disappointed with exhibitions that had 'few pieces of extraordinary merit'.[41]

It seems likely therefore that public opinion was playing catch-up, and in spite of the private exertions of collectors like Nathaniel Clements, Charlemont and the earl of Moira, the Protestant elite were still blamed for neglecting the fine arts, and in particular for the lack of home-grown artists of great stature working in Ireland, and the failure to attract British and European greats to its shores. Some of their accusers were as practised in incendiary hack-writing as Lewis and Preston. Paul Hiffernan, editor of the anti-Charles Lucas newspaper *The Tickler* blamed the neglect of the fine arts upon the gentry's idle accumulation and spending of their wealth.[42] When added to the comments of embittered artists like James Barry, who wrote in 1798 that 'an Irish artist may think himself well off, if his countrymen are not against him, in order to curry favour for themselves',[43] then it is unsurprising that tourists continued to trot out this mantra.

In recent years the work of Anne Crookshank, the Knight of Glin and William Laffan has done much to upgrade the contribution made by early and mid-eighteenth-century Irish or Irish-based artists such as Charles Collins, John Lewis and James Forrester.[44] However the most renowned figures came to prominence late in the century, and James Barry's success – though admittedly he was based in England – suggests a significant advancement in Irish art. Other Irish luminaries working in the late eighteenth century, though not quite his equal, included Nathaniel Hone, who dared to poke fun of Sir Joshua Reynolds in 'The Conjuror' and the portraitist Hugh Douglas Hamilton. The elite of Protestant Ireland, now happy to take on the British government, had an increased sense of national pride in their cultural achievements. Indeed the outrage that Richard Twiss caused, when he 'abused their Buildings, execrated their Paintings, and ridiculed their Manners' is indicative of a new found pride in Dublin's cultural sphere.[45]

Protestant self-confidence was a key facilitator. Interest was being piqued in the attractions of the wild Irish landscape – though perhaps not to the same extent as in the Lake District, Scotland, or Wales – at a time when it was ceasing to hold fears for landowners. As Protestants began to feel that the country was being tamed by English politeness, so these scenes held less of a threat, and instead became of value as an attraction for tourists. Burke's writing on the sublime offered another perspective on this scenery, as was evidenced in John Bush's vignettes of Co. Wicklow and elsewhere.[46] This partly explains why Dublin Society activists were so eager to see a school of Irish landscape study established.[47] In giving a rather back-handed compliment, Richard Twiss noted: 'I saw an exhibition of pictures in Dublin, by Irish artists; excepting those (chiefly landscapes) by Mr Roberts and Mr Ashford, almost all the rest were detestable.'[48] Similar trends were seen in John O'Keefe's theatrical work, for example *The Wicklow mountains* of 1795, which offered the audience the theme of reconciliation with a wild Irish landscape as the backdrop.[49] This appreciation of Ireland's natural canvas tied in neatly with a shift in patriotic ideals; corruption in government could be equated with fake or overly ornamental scenery.[50] Later tourists were not immune to the attractions of native simplicity. Bowden claimed that he enjoyed the rustic songs of peasants at labour 'with a pleasure that transcended any I had ever felt at Vauxhall'.[51]

Taking a comparable theme a sizeable section of John Ferrar's response to Twiss focused on the sites of old-Irish historical importance that the tourist had not deigned to mention, such as the chapel of King Cormac and the cathedral built by Donald O'Brien, king of Limerick.[52] A gentleman living in Stephen's Green wrote to the *Hibernian Journal* to deride Twiss's handling of classic works on travel and history, and add that he would be equally incapable of appreciating Leland and Charles O'Conor. Even old-Irish cultural rituals were dignified through satire, as anything Twiss was seen to criticize immediately acquired some merit in the eyes of patriotic readers. Thus the wake, though not much liked by more charitable tourists, including Arthur Young, was upgraded through the following fictional Twiss-ism:

> When any of their People die, they have what is called a Wake, which lasts for six days, these six Days are spent in dancing, getting drunk, and singing round the dead Body, which is placed in an upright Posture, with a long Pipe in its Mouth; then they carry it to the Grave with some Thousand Yellers following and preceding it, and every Person who attends and refuses to yell is put into a large Hole, dug so deep that he is sunk up to the chin, in which Posture the whole crowd pitch Stones at his Head until they kill him.[53]

The burying of victims up to the chin in earth, accompanied by facial rearrangements – using a knife rather than stone – was, of course, a technique used by the Whiteboys, and was commented on by Young and Twiss. As he was the 18th-century tourist most severe on Ireland's rural protestors, a Whiteboy wake seemed a peculiarly appropriate invention.[54]

5. The piss-pot tourist

The anti-Twiss reaction in newspaper articles, pamphlets, plays and art, even on the streets of Dublin, was notable for both its ferocity and for its extent. Irish newspapers had spent much of the century devoting little column space to Irish news, and yet here was an issue that did not relate directly to Anglo-Irish politics, or to the parliament on College Green, and it was newsworthy. Extra-parliamentary political culture was coming of age, and print, and particularly the newspaper, would drive forward Irish patriotism. The newspaper would be the key consumer object in the radicalization of Irish politics that occurred in the last three decades of the 18th century. However the Twiss affair took the connection between consumer culture and 'political' life to a new level.

Although the possessions of the majority of Irish inhabitants would usually have been bought for practical or perhaps fashionable reasons, there were items purchased in 18th-century Ireland that were chosen because of their political meaning. From the 1730s the production of political trinkets underwent further development, allowing the politically inclined to show their sympathies or affiliations by purchasing goods or decorative items stamped with one's chosen cause. England saw medals struck to honour Admiral Vernon, a host of Cumberland memorabilia and mementoes celebrating the successes of that popular demagogue John Wilkes. The Dublin populace was just as eager for trinkets decorated with images of Irish heroes, and the beloved William III began to appear on glassware and commemorative consumer goods in the 1730s. Jonathan Swift's likeness was reproduced on medals and handkerchiefs following the Wood's Halfpence dispute, and he referred to this phenomenon in his own poetry:

> When none the DRAPIER's Praise shall sing;
> His signs aloft no longer swing;
> His Medals and his Prints forgotten,
> And all his Handkerchiefs are rotten.[1]

Twiss was not idolized in the manner of Wilkes or Swift, but his tour did spark a comedic variant of this kind of consumption: a chamber pot inscribed with a picture of Richard Twiss at the base, allowing the owner to micturate on the hated tourist. Even if Swift's own rudery was not the direct inspiration, he would surely have approved.

On 9 August 1776 the *Hibernian Journal* reported that

> Several Thousand Groce of Chamber-Pots are now finished at Liverpool, on the Inside of the Bottom of which a most laughable Resemblance of Richard Twiss (that Fellow of the Royal Society, who published a Tour through Ireland) is painted. The Original from which this Device is taken was finished by a celebrated Artist, now in Cork, for the Purpose of thus exhibiting this famous Tour writer in a situation, where his very Likeness cannot avoid undergoing a Disgrace which in *propria personae* he has long merited.[2]

Within days the same notice had appeared in *Faulkner's Dublin Journal, Saunders' News-Letter,* and *Finn's Leinster Journal.*[3] Twiss himself confirmed this story. He wrote that 'these pots were all fabricated, soon after the publication of this book, in Liverpool where a Dublin Alderman sat for *my* picture. Plaster of Paris medals were likewise made from Intaglios by Tassie – on the same subject.'[4] Liverpool may have been the source of the original batch of pots. But a surviving fragment – shown on the cover of this book – indicates that a more hurried consignment was also produced. In this case ready-glazed plain chamber pots were used, with the decoration carefully applied afterwards; perhaps as a rapid response to unexpected consumer demand. The location of the find suggests an association with the World's End Delftware manufactory in Dublin.[5]

The anti-Twiss *objets d'art* tapped into a rich vein of Irish satire. Mr Wicksteed, the manufacturer of the medals, was advised by the *Hibernian Journal* that perhaps his images of Twiss should be 'in Brass, rather than Plaster of Paris; the former conveying a true idea of his Countenance; and being, in many Respects, emblematical of his writings; which, like Brass, may glitter and sound, but can never pass current for Sterling or pure Gold'.[6] Twiss had become Ireland's new William Wood, the would-be minter of brass halfpence, and bête noire of Swift in the 1720s. Elsewhere the Drapier – or at least his poetry – was dug up from the grave to traduce Twiss. The references to brass were common – 'My brazen Front', acknowledged the fictional Twiss[7] – and would have conjured up memories of the evils of Catholicism as well as the hated Halfpence. Preston's first anti-Twiss poem confirmed the connection. His heroine Donna Teresa referred to 'civil brass' and described Irish women as 'that ostrich tribe'; words that echoed those of Swift during the Halfpence dispute, when his Ireland had to 'eat Brass as Ostriches do Iron'.[8] Elsewhere the *Freeman's Journal* published a typically barbed poem by Swift under the banner 'A CHARACTER of RICHARD TWISS' and *Walker's Hibernian Magazine* used lines from Swift against Twiss, and claimed that he deserved to be taken for one of the 'Yahoos'; beings that were mired in excrement.[9]

That Twiss's Spanish tormenter was female is significant, as she symbolized not only injured womanhood, but the way in which the episode had reached outside the male political sphere. William Preston's Twiss poems were partly designed to rouse the indignation of Irish women, just as his *The contrast* of 1780 attempted to shame them into wearing clothes of Irish manufacture.[10] The tack may have worked. Elstob met two women who took up the tourist's comments, one of whom was angry that his unflattering remarks on stout female limbs 'was aimed obliquely at the ladies'.[11] The *Hibernian Journal*'s fake Cambridge letter doubtless added to the sense of injustice. In this case the fictional Twiss dismissed Ireland's women; 'not one in five Hundred of the politest knowing how to read or write, and those that do, employing their Time to counterfeit some Member of Parliament's Hand, that they may frank such Letters as they do write'.[12] According to John Carr this forging of franks accusation was employed by Twiss to revenge 'an unsuccessful application for a frank to an Irish lady of fashion'.[13] Yet it had, wrote Preston, contributed to their skill with pen and ink:

> From forging franks, each pert *Hibernian* Miss
> Converts the quill, and has her fling at Twiss.
> The desp'rate inkhorn arms uncounted throngs
> With puns and posies, anecdote and songs.
> Revenge inspires them in Apollo's spite;
> A *Twiss* provokes; and well, or ill, they write.

That said, there was possibly some truth in Twiss's observation, as in June 1784 the *Volunteer Evening Post* argued that it was 'both mean and absurd' to retain the privilege of franking as 'it is most shamefully abused.' The government-supporting newspaper noted that 'counterfeiting is arrived at so daring a height, that there are great numbers, and many of them Ladies of Fashion, who, not content with franking for themselves and friends, keep a kind of public office to supply all who send'. They issued up to 5–10 dozen a day.[14]

Nevertheless, Twiss's attack upon the impoliteness of Irish womanhood gave the go-ahead for Irish women to be really ill-mannered. A motto that differs from the rhyme painted on the surviving shard was supposedly composed for the chamber pots by Ann Whaley, later Lady Clare:

> Here you may behold a liar,
> Well deserving of hell-fire:
> Every one who likes may p____
> Upon the learned Doctor T____[15]

Her mocking lines were soon accompanied by a flurry of splendidly spiteful invective written by patriotic Irish men, and no doubt, women, all celebrating this much sought after consumer item. A verse from a sonnet offered:

> Since he's fled, each CHAMBER-POT,
> Shall the Image bear of Twiss,
> That all who love their native Spot
> On his Booby face may p-ss.[16]

These political piss-pots caught the public imagination, and they were quick to spread throughout Ireland. On 22 August Arthur Young wrote from Strokestown, Co. Roscommon, to tell Caldwell of Twiss's scatological stoneware: 'That poor wight has got his head in the Dublin Chamber services with a ludicrous Inscription – Thus it is to be a Traveller in Ireland.'[17] The following month saw Adams Kearns of North Street, Belfast, hawk his 'Earthenware, printed, enamelled, and plain – CHAMBER POTS, on each of which are those prints of DICK TWISS receiving a deserved punishment for his scandalous lying Tour he wrote and published through this kingdom'. Kearns boasted that he would beat the Dublin price by one shilling.[18] The *Londonderry Journal* printed a poetic epitaph for the tourist, referencing a slang term that would soon be overtaken in Ireland:

> What needs he, therefore, an inscription,
> A Jordan gives him full description.
> I pray you condescend to p-ss
> O'er the remains of Dicky Tw-ss.[19]

Twiss's surname – in a society and period that loved punning – was somewhat unfortunate and was put to other scatological uses. The *Hibernian Journal* reported: 'In such great contempt is the Name of Twiss held in this city, that on the Commode Closet Doors in the working Rooms of the House of Industry, his Name is in Capitals.'[20]

The use of scatology as the primary weapon during this campaign had a number of historical precedents, even in terms of female involvement. Juvenal used the chamber pot for satirical effect, referring to the Amazonian matrons of Rome, who 'squat on the pot'; even in public they were 'squirting like siphons'.[21] Alexander Pope used scatology to attack sub-standard and immoral writers.[22] Most obviously there was a deliberate echo of Swift, that most pungent of punsters. Swift frequently employed scatology to undermine superiority and status. In the *Legion Club* 'Dear Companions hug and kiss, Toast old Glorious in your Piss'.[23] More famously he applied scabrous rhyming to the pristine image of woman:

> For, while the bashful Sylvan Maid,
> As half asham'd, and half afraid,
> Approaching, finds it hard to part
> With that which dwelt so near her Heart.[24]

Preston, in *An heroic answer, from Richard Twiss*, also used the juxtaposition of female innocence and excremental imagery

> They grace the closet, by the couch they stand,
> And, night and morning, load the fairest hand.
> Without, a foliage crowns the polish'd frames,
> And burnish'd gold on flowers of purple flames;
> Within, the potter plants thy Richard's face,
> And bids him stare, in horrible grimace.
> Thro' lakes of amber as the face appears,
> The face repentant seems bedew'd with tears.[25]

Comedy is paramount in his mockery of a very childish approach to women, but there is inevitably a degree of empowerment. In Swift's 'The lady's dressing room' Strephon is appalled by his discovery of Celia's chamber pot, and by fouling his hand in the pan. In the anti-Twiss poems Irish women were strengthened by their earthy qualities; there were no goddesses, nymphs or sylvan maids in Dublin.[26] Just as Swift's Chloe, in his poem 'Strephon and Chloe', was treated to a 'Rouzer' of urine in the face, so was Richard Twiss, and he must have enjoyed these 'lakes of amber' many times over.[27] Indeed for some the picture was not sufficient:

> I'll wash the dirty figure clear,
> But wish th' ORIGINAL was here.
> Did but that scoundrel meet my sight,
> I'd piss upon him, by this light![28]

Twiss's attacks were offensive and hurtful, but scatology allowed not only a much needed national purging, but also a note of levity. The many reminders of the tourist's bodily functions – and thus his imperfections – pricked the pomposity of his prose. Even more satisfying was the base feeling of triumph that came with comparing Ireland's vile calumniator to urine and ordure. As so much tourist tattle focused upon Irish uncleanliness, this was a wonderfully appropriate mode of revenge. In this sense scatology can be seen as the literary equivalent of the lower orders besmirching Twiss's text with soot – or dirt. Indeed scatology offered a link between popular and elite culture; a link that may have had implications for the spread of a more general patriotic spirit.[29]

Thanks to Swift's legacy the potency of scatological satire in later 18th-century Ireland should not be underestimated. It was a means of tapping into past patriotic successes.

As we shall see in chapter six, Twiss's amorousness, whether toward Spanish gypsies or Irish maidens, was a complicated issue to satirize. The chamber-pot offered a very base way around empowering the tourist with sexual potency, and thus Leonard MacNally, by far the most risqué of the anti-Twiss poets, used the device to suggest sexual deviancy, perhaps even coprophilia. In *An answer to a poetical epistle* the tourist had managed to find his way into the beds of the women of Ireland, but not quite in the way that he had hoped:

> And Prudes themselves, rejecting modest Dread,
> Think upon Twiss, and take me into Bed.
> To each pert Fop, the Women show their Faces,
> Kinder to me, – expose their A-s
> And Nelly sitting on her Chamber P-t,
> What see I then? Ye Gods! What see I not?

This point was confirmed in a fictional footnote by 'Richard Lewis', suggesting that piss-pots for ladies should be made with a bandage around the tourist's eyes.[30] Mark Elstob, touring in 1779, or perhaps diligently copying at home, was struck with a similar thought, and perhaps here we may speculate that his words owed as much to Leonard MacNally as they did to Twiss; again showing the wide-ranging impact of anti-Twiss publications for Irish tourism. Elstob remarked: 'His mouth is open to receive the stream … but his eyes too are open … and this it was that entertained me.' Like MacNally, Elstob hinted at a sadomasochistic dimension to the ritual; further debasing the tourist by suggesting that he might take pleasure from the act: 'Mr Twiss must surely acknowledge his great obligation to the condescending ladies who use him so freely, and deign to treat him with such showers of affability'. But Elstob remained a lone Twiss supporter, even in sexual shenanigans, and he imagined a more equitable form of watersports: 'Was he to start up in person – he might immediately return the compliment, if the sudden emersion did not too much ruffle the lady's – disposition.'[31] Certain kinds of tour writers – especially those who opted not to leave their Grub Street garrets – occupied the same literary world as struggling poets, playwrights and hacks. Chetwood was a bookseller and published *A poem on the memorable fall of Chloe's p-s pot*, attributed to Swift. Philip Luckombe worked first as a printer and then for London booksellers. That Elstob should echo MacNally was thus no more surprising than Derrick, Twiss and Young taking up with the likes of Faulkner, Howard and Caldwell.

Irish writers constructed layer upon layer of satire in pieces that delighted in their self-referential form. Fabrication was piled upon fabrication, and a clear lead was taken by prominent Dublin hack writers like Lewis and Preston, and by the city's patriotic organs. They were certainly in on the stunt at the very beginning – early August 1776. Thomas Weekes, a writer involved in Dublin's legal world, and connected to Lewis and Gorges Howard, penned an epigram in response to a letter – possibly fictional – from Twiss on 16 August to the committee for conducting the free press, a non-corporeal body closely associated with the *Freeman's Journal*. The Twiss communication mentioned an order of 10,000 chamber pots, one of which acted as a very peculiar looking glass for the versifier:

> Methinks you've made my phiz too large,
> Your small siz'd looking glass to fit in.
> I can't receive a full discharge
> Unless tis wide enough to shit in.[32]

Weekes's – admittedly extempore – lines once again had Twiss craving something more than the usual odorous stream.

Yet, as Jonathan Swift had demonstrated, the contents of a piss-pot could be used as a sexual spoiler as well as a stimulant. In 'Strephon and Chloe' and 'The lady's dressing room' he was condemning unrestrained passion. The Irish press took heed, depicting Twiss as a lover betrayed by his bodily functions.[33] The *Freeman's Journal* published two poems alleging that when the cowardly Twiss read Richard Lewis's *Defence of Ireland* his intestinal discomfort was such that the accompanying noxious gasses drove his lady companions from the room:

> On receiving the bundle poor Twiss turns pale,
> In a moment bright wit and vivacity fail.
> Tho' lately so joyous, with females engag'd,
> His mind on the rack some misfortune presag'd.
> Deep groan'd his intestines. How cou'd he contain,
> Inly tortur'd by Lewis's merciless strain;
> Whose satire can sink to confusion and shame,
> The snakes who his country betray or defame.
> He wriggled and twisted; – a vapour, like wind,
> Soft murmuring, escap'd, half suppress'd from behind.
> To speak the plain truth without fib or device;
> No lady, court-bred, could have farted so nice.

In fact, as another scribbler graphically related, his predicament was even more mortifying:

> The stink and noise would fright bold men; –
> How then could Ladies stay?
> Quick from the sh-tten hero then
> They frighted, ran away.[34]

These lines also offered a spin on Swift's 'The problems'. In this poem three mistresses of a lecher were waiting for a fart – they being as filthy of mind and habit as he. Twiss, though labelled a lecher, had no like-minded female acquaintances, which again distanced the tourist from polite society.[35] More obviously these poems emphasized Twiss's cowardice – at a time when Ireland's obsession with martial manliness was nearing its peak. In his piss-pot Twiss was the passive receiver, and in this sense he was unmanned. This was why in the anonymous anti-North ministry poem *Fidêfract* Twiss was destined to go searching in vain for Hippocrene, his own fountain. On finding it he would have been required to drink deep – this time of a liquid associated with horses – but he would have found a muse and a means of fighting back.[36]

Of course Twiss was not the first 18th-century tourist to experience bowel problems, as Matthew Bramble in Tobias Smollett's *The expedition of Humphry Clinker*, published in 1771, suffered acutely during the English leg of his jaunt.[37] As with the fictional Twiss it was an encounter with the Celtic periphery that acted as a purgative. *Finn's Leinster Journal* exhibited mock concern over Ireland's apothecaries increasing the price of a popular laxative, 'as all the people of Ireland and elsewhere intend taking it … for the pleasure of ornamenting that false, detestable, and would be tour writer, oftener than nature required.'[38] They may have been superfluous, as one wag claimed that the chamber pot – or rather the picture in it – acted as an evacuant, thus provoking a noisome torrent:

> For when that scoundrel's print you seize,
> You may not strain, but p-ss with ease;
> Nay, should you have a vile ch-dee,
> The sight of Twiss will set you free,
> Will give to your just rage a glow,
> And make your urine freely flow.[39]

In some ways the piss-pot was the perfect anti-English weapon for the Irish, as it was popularly believed that 'The stomach of the Irish went & came', whereas that of the constipated English 'came and stayed.'[40] This time, however, it was the Irish who boasted firm control over their innards. The most prolific of the scatological scribes styled himself 'Rigdum Funnidos', after the plain-speaking courtier in Henry Carey's burlesque play *Chrononhotonthologos* of 1734. In this work Funnidos was needed as an antidote to both pomposity and the Queen's chronic diarrhoea.[41]

These comedic chamber pots ensured that Twiss's infamy lasted until the end of the century. As one perspicacious writer put it in 1776: 'So Twiss's Name shall never be forgot, His Likeness ever in the Chamber-Pot.'[42] The fireside tourist Philip Luckombe, gave his book a spark of originality when he noted that whilst in Ireland in 1779, 'I was frequently presented with the picture of a late Tourist at the bottom of the chamber-pots, with his mouth and eyes open ready to receive the libation'.[43] De Latocnaye, visiting Ireland in 1796, found that the Irish had determined 'childishly, to represent him [Twiss] pictorially in a very undignified position', and in December 1799 *Characters* recalled that Mr Twiss's writings 'Gall-fraught, rous'd the nation's ire, and every dame Within her lowliest vessel stamp'd his front.'[44] In addition there was proof that the printing trade was part of an Atlantic world. John Cozine's poem *Dick Twiss* published in New York in 1780 used the image of Twiss as a lover secreted in the chamber pot. And Twiss's name turned up in a number of American periodicals and newspapers during the nineteenth century. A Boston periodical recollected Ireland's peculiar revenge on Twiss in 1821, and anecdotes relating to Twiss's travels also appeared in New York and Philadelphia publications.[45]

More impressively, Twiss had found a place in the popular vernacular. Luckombe remarked that 'the utensil now is more frequently called by the name of a Twiss than any other, in contempt of the illiberal reflections of that gentleman, who was so hospitably received here.'[46] Shitty soubriquets also crossed the Irish Sea, as in 1811 the London-published *Dictionary of the vulgar tongue* offered 'Twiss' as a slang term for a chamber pot.[47] Robert Jephson may have been rekindling the mischief-making of the 1770s when, in 1794, he asserted that Twiss was known as 'TUMBLE-DUNG' in England thanks to his words on that beetle in a work of natural history. The 'tumble–dung' beetle also featured in his Spanish tour and Preston's *An heroic epistle*. Jephson, as scabrous on Twiss's French tour as his hack colleagues had been on his Irish writings, added, 'would not one imagine he was rendering back the reeking streams his effigy had inhaled at the bottom of so many chamber-utensils in Ireland?'[48] Thanks to Jephson – who Twiss had once praised – he had made the ultimate scatological transformation: the tourist was now a gatherer of excrement and his works were urine. Again there is a Swiftian echo as the dean had referred to bad writing as 'excremental'.[49]

Twiss, though, was not the only individual to suffer the ignominy of finding himself associated with this essential consumer item. Dr Henry Sacheverell, another figure much-hated in Ireland – at least by those of a whiggish inclination who reacted violently against his anti–dissenting sermons of 1709 – apparently appeared in portrait form at the base of chamber pots. The profits accruing from this venture were such that the potter was able to finance the building of a house – 'Piss Pot Hall' – in Clapton, near Hackney.[50] Colonel Sir John Blaquiere, an able politician but disliked intensely by patriot MPs, was allegedly accorded a similar honour. A correspondent of the *Hibernian Journal* claimed that the same ingenious artist to whom the Public are already so much obliged for supplying a convenient Word to express a certain necessary utensil, is now very busily employed in finishing, in the same masterly manner, a Number of Pans for close-stools, which, hereafter are to be called QUIERS; and as there is an evident similarity between COLONEL CRIB-ACRE and the TOUR-WRITER, the one being in Politics exactly what the other appeared in Print, and both equally offensive to Ireland, he considers it but Justice to hand them together, with equal Marks of Distinction to Posterity.[51]

Blaquiere was identified as a doppelganger for Twiss's personal corruption – he had already been lampooned in one of the anti-Twiss poems[52] – and had to suffer a portion of his name becoming a nickname for chamber pots throughout Ireland. If true then the *Hibernian Journal* undoubtedly played an important role in popularizing both the items and their label. Blaquiere's name was still associated with 'jobbing and dirt of every kind' in 1784, a reference to his support for the unpopular paving bill of that year.[53] A third Irish individual to be associated with this practice was Lord Balfour.[54] However the chamber pot with accompanying image was not restricted to Britain and Ireland. United Irish literature referred to a French republican ready to use a piss-pot with an open-mouthed Louis XVI at the base.[55]

Although very much a frivolous item, it can be argued that success of the Twiss chamber pots paved the way for a more obviously political form of consumerism. In the early 1780s mementoes of Volunteering such as oil paintings, engravings, medals, and pottery and glassware with suitable motifs, were sold throughout Ireland. The United Irishmen also cottoned on to the notion that politics was a mass-marketable commodity and produced trinkets to help get their message across. These items made it possible for all sections of the Irish populace to buy into a political identity. Yet though the Twiss-pots offer a convenient symbol of this episode, they should not overshadow the items that really made the affair, and created any post-Twiss political legacy: newspapers, pamphlets and books, and the accompanying ephemera produced by Dublin's printers and hacks.

6. Twiss and the formation of Irish identity

Ireland's political elite – exclusively Protestant – had spent much of the 18th century exhibiting a siege-like mentality, most obviously expressed through the Penal Laws. The late 1770s and early 1780s would see significant steps towards liberalizing the world view of the Protestant elite; restrictions on Catholics were eased, and some Catholics were even permitted to buy into Irish patriotism through membership of the Volunteers. It was an auspicious moment for the publication of a tour that so knowingly cast aspersions on the Irish character and identity. Of course many tourists determined to find fault with their destinations, and they undermined local inhabitants, customs and mores as a means of bolstering their own sense of self and, more importantly, the superiority of their homeland.[1] An unusual side-effect of the Twiss case, however, is that a tour actually played a role – however minor – in formulating a more inclusive version of an Irish identity. For a transitory moment Twiss's *A tour in Ireland* gave Dublin's Protestant elite an opportunity to find new allies in parts of Ireland – most notably Connacht – where they might not have considered looking ten years earlier. This may have initially been a carefully cultivated squabble between Twiss and Dublin's publishers and hack writers, but it had much wider ramifications.

When visiting Cork, Bowden noted that its inhabitants were 'eminently advanced in the arts of industry'.[2] As usual Twiss was able to make a similar observation much more insulting. He argued that 'the *forte* of the citizens does not lie in the sciences of painting, sculpture, architecture, music, or such trifles, but in the more essential arts relative to eating and drinking; such as the slaughter of hogs, oxen, and sheep, in order to exchange the superfluous pork, beef, and mutton, for wine'.[3] Twiss then associated Cork's residents with impoliteness, lack of material and artistic culture and an unrestrained appetite for alcohol. The majority of the inhabitants of Cork were Catholics, and thus these traits might have been connected in Twiss's mind with Catholicism and the 'old' Irish. Yet just as elite Protestant views on the 'old' Irish metamorphosed during this period, so did attitudes towards certain aspects of their consumer and material culture. Irish buttermilk, for example, had 'old'-Irish impolite connotations, but also health-giving properties, partly due to the perceived robustness of the Irish peasantry. This image existed alongside that of the English or Irish macaroni, whose effeminate drink of choice was milk.[4]

It is an exemplar suggestive of the themes that inform the final chapter of this study: an examination of the ways in which the reaction to Twiss's *A tour in Ireland* illustrated shifts in the nature of Irish Protestant identity. In his criticisms of Ireland's material culture and its impoliteness, he was striking at the heart of Ascendancy Ireland. In Dublin, Ireland's elite had started to fashion a capital worthy of the title of second city of the British empire. The ability of Ireland's writers and artists was now being lauded with patriotic fervour, and the press expressed disappointment at the elite's willingness to pass over Irishmen in favour of foreign (English and continental) talent. That Twiss's attack on Protestant material culture should raise hackles amongst Ireland's elite is perhaps unsurprising. What is more interesting is that Dublin commentators might leap to the defence of sections of the Irish people who in the past might have been accused of retarding the progress of the civilizing mission. In a number of areas writers took on board Twiss's criticisms, even embraced them, and turned them into a weapon with which they could attack both the tourist and notions of Englishness. These themes can be divided into two specific traits associated with an 'old'-Irish identity. First, a tendency towards aggressive behaviour; a roguish character that at its most extreme was connected with a propensity for duelling and a willingness to abduct heiresses. Secondly, excessive forms of consumption, be it food or drink, summed up in the phrase 'lavish hospitality'.

Whether or not duelling in Ireland has been exaggerated, and it does seem as though it has,[5] the quarrelsome, duelling Irishman was an important part of the image of the Irish – including the more recent Protestant arrivals – that was consumed by the British in novels, plays, and newspapers. In a rare concession, Richard Twiss said that 'a prudent traveller may as easily avoid any such disagreeable encounters there, as elsewhere.' Though even here Twiss could take little solace in a good deed done, as his words were quickly rehashed by a newspaper, reappearing as the following comment on Irish men: 'They drink Whiskey Punch until they are so inebriated as to be divested of all Reason, and then, when all true Courage is asleep, they deliberately go out and shoot at one another. This they call Duelling.'[6] If Twiss had been in credit with the Irish reader for his moderate comments on duelling, this was small beer compared to his labelling the inhabitants of Connacht as 'savage'. And along with his unflattering description of the legs of Irish women, it allowed Irish commentators to respond to Twiss on the question of personal and national manliness.

Rather than see his slights as an attack on a certain unloved section of the Irish populace, Dublin Protestants realized Swift's misleading appeal *To the whole people of Ireland*, and regarded themselves as equal victims with their Catholic brethren. Much of the post-publication backlash touched upon the subject of manliness, and commentary on Twiss's own sexual predilections took two forms. His Spanish tour made it very clear that he delighted in female company, at least of a certain kind: visiting a convent near Zamora he found 'no more than eight ladies, all old and ugly, so that I made my visit as short as possible'. He was accused, therefore, of having a lascivious eye for young women.[7] This foible had struck observers in the Grantham circle. A disapproving Waddilove, summarizing the book of the Spanish tour for Grantham, reported: 'he says he generally spent the Evenings with Ladies … next door to the Inn where he lodged'.[8] Richard Lewis had obviously noted the same passage. One of the perks of his Spanish tour, he remarked, was that 'in every Inn he found a *Mistress*'.[9]

Commenting on Twiss's Irish trip *Walker's Hibernian Magazine* claimed that he was regularly turned out of company for behaving with indecency to the ladies. According to a correspondent of the *Hibernian Journal*, 'a Right Rev. Gentleman' ordered Twiss 'to be publicly turned out of Company at Mallow', and John Ferrar confirmed that the archbishop of Tuam had ordered Twiss to be removed from the gathering.[10] On another occasion he had 'the impudence to draw the ladies to a window, to exhibit to them a parcel of obscene pictures'. He was also said to have been ill-behaved at the Nenagh assembly.[11] An anonymous poet in the *Freeman's Journal* claimed that he introduced 'himself among Ladies of the first distinction here, with a song of baudy'.[12] Furthermore, according to Preston's commentary, 'Mr Twiss had seriously conceived a design of making a catalogue of beauties, ranked according to their respective merits, for the embellishment of his intended book of travels through Ireland.'[13]

Though we might assume that this kind of behaviour would not have dented Twiss's reputation in England, it sat oddly with preconceived notions on the chastity of Irish women. Even Twiss acknowledged that in Ireland 'debauching a married woman or a single woman is one of the greatest crimes it is possible to commit'. He added: 'galantry, or intrigue, is but little carried on in Ireland, and a Cicisbeo (in the libertine sense of the word) is here almost as unknown as a snake'.[14] Opinion on Twiss's amorous adventures was also likely to be shaped by the rather complicated model of 18th-century masculinity, as discussed by David M. Weed in reference to James Boswell. On the one hand male sexual desire was licensed, but self-control was also vital, 'so that it does not lead to the excesses that dissipate a man and render him effeminate'.[15]

The image of Twiss as an amorous tourist was not entirely suitable to patriotic Dublin writers. He could be criticized for exploiting the inexperienced and being obliged to pay for sex – wishing to view 'what Whores possess'[16] – but a much more potent line of attack was to suggest that his true sexual interests did not lie with women. Even before the publication of Twiss's *A tour in Ireland*, Irish patriots enjoyed levelling charges of effeminacy and homosexuality at their ministerial enemies, much helped by the fact that in England, the Irishman, along with the African male, was regarded as a particularly potent sexual figure.[17] Such rumour mongering was an important weapon in the patriot opposition's armoury, and during the Money Bill dispute Archbishop George Stone's close relationship with Lord George Sackville gave patriot satirists plenty of opportunities for homophobic jibes; physical vices being equated with political corruption. Anti-Stone toasts included: 'May he that does not have a Woman, be transported to the Isle of Man' and 'May back-lane never get the better of Bride-street'.[18] Sackville – the 'buggering hero', according to John Wilkes and Charles Churchill – appeared in Preston's poem on the evacuation of Boston thanks to his position as American Secretary. He continued to be characterized by 'boyish pertness', but having left aside his 'parasite' and 'whore' he drew his 'bodkin spear' to do battle with the Americans.[19]

Many of the articles, poems and dramatic pieces that appeared on Twiss, a bachelor, focused on his unmanliness. Richard Lewis described him as 'the Prince of lettr'd Coxcombs', 'a Macaroni Traveller and Beau', and as 'a prating, forward, vain, conceited, creature'.[20] A satirical interlude performed in Belfast's Mill Street Theatre in April 1778 was titled 'Twiss in Ireland; or, the fop in disgrace'.[21] In Europe it was said that he was 'scorn'd by ev'ry Boy and Miss', and he was supposedly physically thrashed by an Irishman in a London coffee-house.[22] The *Hibernian Journal* reported that during his visit to Algiers, his 'Mahometan master' caused him to be deprived of the 'little Manhood' he had. It was also pointed out that there was no way he could have asserted that Irish women had thick legs, as he had no knowledge of them other than seeing them walking.[23] Similarly when he quoted the Scottish traveller William Lithgow's comments on the breasts of Irish women: 'very fit to be made money bags for East or West Indian merchants, being more than halfe a yard long, and as wel wrought as any tanner in the like charge, could ever mollifie such leather', he was damned both for repeating the slander and for the footnote – spotted by the ever-alert Lewis – 'I never saw any such breasts.'[24] Flagellation tropes were particularly common, such as in a satirical print of 1776 titled: *The devil take the hindmost; or, Dicky Twiss's method of travelling post through Ireland.* Bloomfield's caricature showed Twiss 'receiving chastisement for his Impertinence to a very worthy Family, at Mallow, where he had been most hospitably entertained'. It was also perhaps a reference to Twiss's own comments upon modes of travel on the Iberian peninsula, in this case the use of sharp sticks to prod jack-asses.

Despite a paucity of material, Dublin's anti-Twiss writers were astonishingly creative. Apart from the occasional quip directed at the manners of Irish men and women, Twiss's encounters with the fashionable world did not feature prominently in his tour. Yet it provided the press with a launch-pad for an attack on Macaroni fashions and modish behaviour in Dublin. Its hero was another tourist, the counterpoint to Twiss, Connacht man Cornelius O'Dowde.

The *Hibernian Journal* had a good deal of fun with the fictional Co. Sligo squire. After a visit from a frizeur, O'Dowde was told by his cousin that his hair 'was so much in Taste, that I might venture to look out of the window into the street, provided I did not show any part of my Body.' But despite his rustic manners the reader's sympathy stays firmly with O'Dowde, '[c]onfined to my room for want of Cloaths to appear as a Man of Taste.' In another episode fashionable whims were shown to erode political steadiness, and O'Dowde had no truck with his cousin's suggestion that he changed his opinions on the American war depending upon the company.[25] O'Dowde also attacked the oversized bag-wigs that were all the rage amongst Dublin's fashionable ladies, referring to 'the Filthiness of loading her Brains and deforming her Beauty with such Additions of borrowed locks oftentimes taken from envenomed Sculls'. However the principal trope that emerges relates to masculinity, and O'Dowde was discomforted by his new image. He could not see the need for 'small-clothes prodigiously wide', as he never had the need to magnify his manhood in the past.[26]

Constrained, even hamstrung, by the regulations of polite Dublin society, O'Dowde was on his best behaviour. Other Connacht men appearing in the wider drama fitted more neatly with tourist stereotypes of the Irishman as a little 'flashy', especially after a drink.[27] Twiss's effeminacy was thus contrasted with the brutal masculinity of the Irishman: 'Despis'd by the Women, and drubb'd by the Men.'[28] And so the invectives written by patriot commentators were as likely to laud Irish aggressive manliness, as they were to hint at Twiss's homosexuality. The Limerick printer John Ferrar claimed that 'a young man in Cashell broke Twiss's violin on his head, for saying that there was not a good practical musician in Ireland, or a man that had any ear for music.'[29] Lewis urged Ireland's 'strong-back'd [sedan] Chairmen' to take revenge upon Twiss.[30] Preston wrote: 'Where'er you tread, the snares of death surround; Fierce is the duellist, the punk unfound.' Even the women of 'old' Ireland were, it seems, a match for Twiss:

> Hibernian dames are train'd to cuff and kick,
> And nature arm'd them, – for their legs are thick.
> The thirst of vengeance ev'ry breast inspires,
> And bowls of whiskey feed their cruel fires.[31]

The rumour that whilst in Ireland he was 'often kicked out of Company for Impertinence,' and the determination of the men of Connacht to exact revenge upon the tourist, resulted in a series of stories, squibs and satirical prints that played amusingly upon the stereotype drawn by Twiss: to the English writer's cost. Twiss was warned: 'Trust not dear Dick, your Foot on Irish Ground; vengeance is out'.[32] John Ferrar predicted that the tourist would 'wander about in constant fear, for as there are Irishmen in every part of the world, he will certainly meet the chastisement his insolence deserves.'[33] In the *Hibernian Journal* it was reported that 'three or four of those Savages, whom this Fellow mentions to dwell in Connaught, lately appeared in London; of which notice being given to the Traveller, he instantly bid adieu to England – not being able to stand the shock – or perhaps fearing what he was conscious he so richly deserved – a *Horsewhipping*.'[34] The newspaper also noted that 'two Gentlemen of landed property, in the province of Connaught, have publicly declared they will directly follow that infamous scoundrel Twiss, through whatever Country in which he may take shelter, until they make him, in his own handwriting, recant every syllable of that slanderous Production (his Tour through Ireland) or fight them on the Spot.'[35] William Preston's Twiss had nightmares about Connacht: 'And oaken cudgels whistle in the wind, And sharp-toed shoes assail me from behind.'[36]

The image of the rambunctious Connacht man had already played an important role in Dublin's political culture, as the Co. Galway-born E. Kelly had assumed the leadership of the anti-Thomas Sheridan faction in the violent gentlemen versus players dispute. Helen Burke suggests that this particular affair had a sectarian dimension.[37] In both cases there was a clash between Connacht and the new polite world, with this predominantly Catholic province standing for older, often impolite, forms of behaviour, and, more particularly, traditional, and very assertive, modes of masculinity. Other tourists saw the newly-planted Irish being infected with these 'old'-Irish attitudes. In 1773 Burrows observed: 'There must be something very pleasant in savage manners' as little could 'prevent every Colony of the English from degenerating, from mixing with, and adopting' Irish modes of behaviour.[38]

The Twiss episode indicates that some writers were happy to play along with this, and in doing so they were tapping into a vogue for primitivism, reflected in Gabriel Beranger's comparisons between Ireland and Tahiti.[39] According to the *Hibernian Journal* Twiss was tracked down in London and repaid for his impertinence; a task rendered easier by this newspaper's willingness to inform its readers that he was a regular at Smyrna's Coffee-House in St James's Street.[40] It seemed that 'Mr K—, a Gentleman well known in the polite world, and who owns a considerable property in the province of Connaught, met the noted Twiss, a few weeks since, at a coffee-house in London.' The gentleman in question asked Twiss whether he remembered 'what Account you gave of the Inhabitants of Connaught, and that you believed that Part of Ireland was inhabited by savages?' Twiss replied, 'Something similar to it'. The newspaper reported that the Connacht gentleman then,

looking him steadfastly in the Face, said, 'I give you credit for being so candid, Mr Twiss, and to convince you that your Judgment, in Respect to Connaught, is *well-founded*. I can tell you that I am one of those savages whom you have so *truly* denominated; and not being able to get rid of my native Ferocity, although surrounded by so many well bred Gentlemen as I see here, I feel myself inclined to give you a sensitive Demonstration of our savage wildness'. On concluding which words, he fell on our miserable tour Writer, and tore his Face in such a manner, as to leave a Crimson streak from each Spot where the Nails of his Fingers first entered. After thus disciplining the unhappy Twiss, according to the Fellow's own wanton Idea of Connaught, Mr K— took him by the Nose, beat him round the Coffee-Room with an Oaken Saplin, and then kicked him out to the Street, to the great Astonishment of all the Gentlemen present. When this Business was finished, (for which the whole Nation stand largely indebted to their champion) Mr K— sat down.

After this, one or two gentlemen present said that it was unfair to attack a man in such a manner without his sword. The Connacht gentleman offered to meet any man who wished to defend Twiss at any time using whatever weapons the other chose. Following a general silence, Mr K— waited until the customers had all left the Coffee House, 'and then went Home, conscious of having meritoriously chastened an ignorant, impertinent Puppy, and of having convinced the English, that he who makes unjust Reflections on the Irish, will not long remain unpunished.'[41]

This incident – fictional or non-fictional – gives a useful demonstration of the ways in which gentlemen were willing to take on the characteristics of the 'old' Irish. In this case it was in a mocking way, but it was at the same time defensive, of Irish identity and indeed regional identity. Also of interest is that the *Hibernian Journal* clearly approved of Mr K—'s conduct, despite his unorthodox, and ungentlemanly attack. The veracity of this tale was hinted at in an obituary in the *Belfast News-Letter*. Denis O'Kelly, a Connacht man, was killed in a duel on 15 July 1790. The accompanying report said that he was 'a gentleman of high accomplishment' and 'the most intrepid courage'. He had been, it seems, a capable duellist, having fought the notorious Beauchamp Bagenall among others. More importantly the flattering report stated that, 'To his hand was Mr Twiss, the itinerant calumniator of this country, indebted for the horse-whipping he received some years since at a coffee-house in London, as the reward of his aspersions on the people of Ireland.'[42] Presumably the encounter with O'Kelly must have made Twiss regret his former willingness to accept that the Irish predisposition towards drinking and duelling was a myth.

Twiss received a report of the same obituary printed in the *Times* from his friend Francis Douce, who termed it libellous but neglected to enclose a copy of the article in his letter. Twiss later reflected: 'is the paragraph actionable? I am told not, as I can prove no Damages.'[43] A jaundiced Twiss later complained: 'our papers are all lies', and he referred to the *General Magazine* as an 'execrable publication' and the *Gentleman's Magazine* as 'vile'.[44] After a reference to his 'chastisement' was made in an Irish Commons debate in the *Morning Post*, he cut the offending section out, stuck it in his private copy of the tour, and scrawled a denial that he had met with any chastisement.[45] In some ways it matters not whether the Kelly horsewhipping was fictional. The obituary shows that some of the tales of 1776 were believed and had entered the popular consciousness; to such an extent that real faces could be put to fictional deeds and that they would last the test of time. In this light the power of Dublin's printers should not be underestimated.

In his *An heroic answer, from Richard Twiss*, William Preston created a fictional travel-writer, wearing 'ass's ears' and clutching 'a mighty stink-pot', who warned Twiss that he had been undone by his 'ill-manners'; an indication of the punishment awaiting the visitor who accepted Ireland's famed hospitality and then criticized its efforts.[46] The nature of Irish consumption, often cited by contemporary commentators as excessive, lavish or simply impolite, gave further scope for a deliberate repositioning of Protestant Irish identity. Twiss had launched a vitriolic attack upon the material culture of the Irish, and in particular that of the 'old' Irish. For example Twiss was concerned that mistaken largesse in the treatment of Irish daughters meant that 'men of moderate fortunes cannot afford to maintain them in the style to which they were bred or *reared*'; a point that was echoed by Bowden.[47] Preston allowed Twiss to pacify Donna Teresa accordingly:

> Fear not a rival on th' Hibernian plain;
> I scorn its damsels, a penurious train.
> Scarce by their portions are their gowns supply'd,
> And all their little wealth is dress and pride.[48]

Elsewhere, in reference to the Irish lower orders, Twiss commented that 'shoes and stockings are seldom wore by these beings, who seem to form a distinct race from the rest of mankind'.[49] In this he was prefigured by Derrick, and followed by Luckombe and Carr. Twiss had most likely read the latter as he penned the following annotation in his personal copy of the tour, echoing a comment by Carr on Kerry: 'I am informed that in the northern parts of Ireland, the dogs bark at every stranger they see who wears breeches. It is said that women taught the dogs this trick.'[50] Newspapers were quite happy to invent further slurs, deliberately ratcheting up the tension. In the fictional Cambridge letter the tourist recounted: 'The common People are merely Savages; they eat and drink like Beasts, and seldom have any covering but a coarse dirty Shirt.' As for their farmers, they live 'like the common Wretches, in Dirt and Nastiness'.[51] In the light of comments by Twiss and others, such a missive would surely have rung true. Burrows had found that 'the nastiness of the Irish of all ranks is inconceivable'.[52] But the Cambridge letter was mockery that had patriotic intent, and as such it can be linked to Carole Fabricant's notion of the 'anti-tourist'. In his *A short view of the state of Ireland* Swift's language is certainly redolent of the tourist genre, describing farmers 'living in Filth and Nastiness upon Buttermilk and Potatoes, without a Shoe or Stocking to their Feet'.[53] Edmund Burke also picked out the uncomfortable and the ugly. He confused cabins with dunghills; finding inside 'Men, Women, Children, Dogs, and Swine lying promiscuously'.[54] But the broader satiric intent in these works reveals a patriot's empathy and involvement, rather than a tourist's observation and entertainment.

In Twiss's view the 'old' Irish continued to act as a brake on national progress. Commenting on the Catholic peasantry, Twiss observed that 'what little the men can obtain by their labour, or the women by their spinning, is usually consumed in whisky'.[55] Twiss had no expectations of politeness amongst the lower sorts in Ireland, and of course he was not alone. Maria Edgeworth herself made an indirect attack on Twiss and his ilk in her portrayal of the ignorant travel writer, Lord Craiglethorpe, in *Ennui*,[56] but it is clear that she and Twiss actually shared some common ground. Carr, her main target, was indebted to Edgeworth for a comical anecdote on the misuse of hair-pieces as brooms, as well as the 'port if you please' quip.[57]

In more general terms the Protestant elite found it difficult to cast off the reputation for extravagance and lavish hospitality which they had inherited from the 'old' Irish. But, although tourists continued to be critical, Twiss's comments gave rise to something of a reassessment among selected visitors, and, more importantly, the Irish themselves. Robert Gamble, revenue collector, after experiencing the largesse of Sir James Caldwell wrote to his host: it is not rare to meet good cheer in this kingdom, that I will assert in spite of Twiss.'[58] Caldwell also approvingly detailed the fulsome spreads – excepting the quality of pineapples – offered by his friends and acquaintances, but he noted that French style was having an influence: very elegant, with 'few things substantial'.[59] Indeed Dublin writers did much to defend these customs. William Preston referred to 'Their only boast, the hospitable mind', and the *Hibernian Journal* reflected on Twiss's 'Residence in this Land of Hospitality'.[60]

In her *Ennui* Edgeworth's Lady Geraldine complained of the tourist Craiglethorpe: 'here he comes to hospitable, open-hearted Ireland; eats as well as he can in his own country; drinks better than he can in his own country; accepts all our kindness without a word or a look of thanks, and seems the whole time to think, that "Born for his use, we live but to oblige him!"'[61] In contrast Twiss was much criticized in the Irish press for his niggardly disposition. The printer John Ferrar sneered at him for staying in 'a sorry alehouse' in Limerick, for a miserly bill ran up in Killarney, and for subsisting 'chiefly at Gentlemen's tables'.[62] One of the more persuasive potted biographies noted that 'he never made any figure abroad, being always penurious, and grumbling at necessary expences'.[63] In the 1790s Robert Jephson alleged that his positive treatment of France was due to the fact that unlike in London he was awarded a free passport.[64]

Tendency towards lavish entertainments at least distinguished the Irish from the parsimonious Scots, who were the regular butts of Irish wit. Anti-Scottish sentiment was at least as important a theme in Irish patriotic thought as in English; more so in some ways, as Ireland looked jealously at the trade advantages it had gained through union, and Scotland's ungratefulness manifested in the rebellions of 1715 and 1745. In a fake gallows speech Twiss acknowledged that his father was Scottish, Sawney Twiss, who had been in the rebellion, before fleeing to Holland. Meanwhile the *Hibernian Journal* was terming the American conflict a 'Scotch War', had found an insulting lexicon for its readers in the 'Royal Scotch Political Dictionary', and was berating the hapless viceroy Lord Buckinghamshire for adopting the 'strictest Scottish oeconomy' in his management of Dublin Castle; a point that was picked up on by an observant tourist.[65] William Preston included a number of anti-Scots jibes in his *A congratulatory poem on the late successes of the British arms* of 1776 and *The female congress* of 1779, the latter referring to '[t]he voice of gain, which *Scotchmen* always hear.'[66]

More significant in melding Twiss, the Scots and ministerial corruption was the Dublin-published epic poem *Fidéfract* of 1778. This piece, directed at North and his political supporters, was riddled with anti-Scots sentiment, containing hostile references to the absolutist Stuarts, historical betrayals and the ever-multiplying London Scots.[67] But it was also located in Dublin's close-knit worlds of print and politics, hence the references to patriot heroes Grattan and Newenham, government recruits Flood and Hely-Hutchinson, and the writers Amyas Griffith, Preston and Swift. Equally telling is the persistence of the much-loved scatological tropes that dominated the Twiss episode. For example, 'Mac was a Vermin-eaten Log, The pissing Post of ev'ry Dog'. The inability of Scots to disguise their true nature was expressed in, 'So Urine empty'd in a Rill, Is nothing else but Urine still'. And if the readers had still not grasped the connection, this was hammered home with the celebratory: 'Thou who with copious Draughts of P-s, Hast lately elevated TWISS'.[68]

Anti-Scottish sentiment could be tied into parsimony, patriotism and even piss-pots. But the contemporaneous assault by the *Hibernian Journal* upon James Macpherson, the author of the fake Ossian tales, for 'lessening the Merit of our Glorious Deliverer',[69] opened up another angle of attack. Bowden noted Macpherson's prejudice towards Ireland, and from the Irish perspective both Twiss and Macpherson were fabricators, guilty of slandering Irish history and traditions.[70] This explains why a writer in the *Hibernian Magazine* suggested that Twiss's F.R.S. was a more suitable acronym for 'Forger of Romantic Slanders'.[71]

One final point worth making on the anti-Scots trope is that though clearly prevalent in the work of Preston and other Dublin writers, the Ulster-Scots living in the north – in this period a hotbed of radical patriotism – make it dangerous to generalize. Indeed one of the interesting features of the anti-Twiss backlash was the slight regional variations. For example the version of the gallows speech published in the *Londonderry Journal* referred to Twiss's father as 'Richard' rather than 'Sawney' Twiss. Whilst in the *Belfast News-Letter* 'AN IMPARTIAL SCOTSMAN' wrote to condemn the writings of tourists to Scotland and Ireland, and of course looked forward to purchasing his own piss-pot.[72]

In fairness to Twiss he did acknowledge that he had erred in his 'opinion that the inhabitants were addicted to drinking, given to hospitality, and apt to blunder.' He noted that 'hospitality and drinking went formerly hand in hand, but since the excesses of the table have been so judiciously abolished, hospitality is not so violently practiced as heretofore, when it might have been imputed to them as a fault.'[73] But in other ways his malicious commentary on Irish consumption pushed the native and Protestant Irish together. For example most travellers reflected upon the importance of the potato within the diet of the Irish peasantry, and some, including Twiss, alleged that this root vegetable was also beloved by the upper orders. In reference to the gentry, he noted 'the universal use of potatoes, which form a standing dish at every meal; these are eaten by way of bread'. Twiss, as usual, was able to trump the snide comments of other travellers, not for the first time by referring to the practices of the fairer sex: 'even the ladies indelicately placing them on the table-cloth, on the side of their plate, after peeling them.'[74]

William Williams' study of tourism and Irish rural society frequently acts as an apologia for Gaelic customs.[75] But in many ways he was beaten to it by Irish Protestant writers in the 1770s; in Seamus Deane's view this was 'the first Celtic revival'.[76] For example, by the last quarter of the century there were clear signs that the potato was losing its image as a crop beloved of a slothful peasantry, and being embraced as part of a new, more inclusive Irish identity. In the middle of the ferment caused by Twiss's book *Walker's Hibernian Magazine* published 'An essay on potatoes' and included a recipe for potato bread,[77] and *Faulkner's Dublin Journal* urged botanically-minded gentlemen to 'promote and improve the cultivation of this necessary Provision'.[78] Even tourists pitched in, and Bowden offered Irish peasants advice on how to deal with frost-bitten tubers.[79] The potato motif could be used in a very knowing fashion; appropriately enough given the nature of the anti-Twiss response. The gentlemen of Kildare established the 'potatoe stakes', a five guinea race at the

Curragh.[80] More political statements were also possible using this humble national root. The symbolic smearing of Lord Loftus's carriage with potato in November 1771 was reward for siding with Lord Townshend's new Castle party.[81]

In terms of anti-Twiss writing, the embrace of rural 'old-Ireland' is best exemplified in 'Cornelius O'Dowde's *Tour through Dublin*'. 'To be out of the Fashion is as bad as being out of the World', said O'Dowde, 'and a Man under that Circumstance looks as awkward as a Sow with one Ear'. It was no coincidence that the sensible O'Dowde was a Connacht man. The O'Dowdes were a Co. Sligo 'old'-Irish family, and so readers would have recognized Cornelius as a Catholic, or, perhaps more likely, a convert, as O'Dowde happily inherited his father's land and fortune. His foster-brother Denis McDermot's use of the term 'trawneen' (a thing of little importance), also hints at Gaelic Irish antecedents.[82]

7. Conclusion

The anti-Twiss campaign eventually ran out of puff. Though a particularly rich seam of satire, it had been mined to exhaustion. The summer and autumn of 1776 had been quiet news-months with parliament no longer in session. But by mid-October 1776 news of casualties in America and of Howe's campaign were pushing Twiss ephemera out of the news. It is vital that we stress the fact that the reaction to Twiss's tour was a variant of print warfare, conjured by Dublin's printers. There is, I think, a need for caution before ascribing the word 'national' to anti-Twiss feeling. Admittedly it is tempting to see Twiss, a member of the loyal Hans Town Association in the 1790s, ideologically opposed to his former Irish foes; his tour was one of the most uncharitable of a genre that Clare O'Halloran sees as a 'form of colonial literature'.[1] The publication of an abridged tour in the rebellion year of 1798 – which saw the murder of William Hamilton, author of a guide to Antrim, in Donegal – was hardly coincidental, and Twiss's anti-Whiteboy comments were highlighted by his new printer, William Mavor, as a warning of the dangers of leniency when dealing with social protest.[2] But the radicalism of Newenham and his admirers in print was not travelling in the direction of United Irish politics. Indeed, according to one Irish writer active in the 1770s, it was Twiss who had radical inclinations. In response to his French tour Robert Jephson alleged that Twiss approved of the ransacking of French churches, defended cannibalism and admired the ferocity of the female revolutionaries.[3] Twiss was, it must be acknowledged, surprisingly positive on aspects of Revolutionary French society, and this applied to changes in politics as well as politeness. Indeed for his Irish edition, perhaps conscious of a radicalized audience, he added the following comment on the storming of the Bastille: 'The majesty of the people was never more conspicuous than on that day.'[4]

Though an Irish cause célèbre, Twiss's tour must also be considered in terms of common responses to modes of touring. Certain kinds of tour and tourist had less than noble ambitions and were treated accordingly. Six years before Twiss, John Bush reflected on the 'dull, stupid, and unnatural method of circulating and zigzagging through all the insignificant towns of every country'.[5] Commenting on Twiss's Spanish tour, Frederick Robinson observed: 'I am quite tired of modern travels which contain but little more information than what & where the writer eat & drank.'[6] And yet Twiss had put a good deal more work into his Spanish travelogue than his book on Ireland, which, according to the author of 'A tour in the south of Ireland' was based on 'getting a few hard terms by rote, and a catalogue of the most famous rarities of nature and art'.[7] An Irish anti-Twiss poet jibed that he was 'A Translator of travels, Relater discreet, Of what ev'ry Porter may see in the Street'.[8] It is significant that the tourist closest in tone to Twiss, John Carr, was also treated to a satirical response.

Though Carr was annoyed, and sued, his tours sold well, and he must have known that his brand of travelogue went down well with the public. When De Latocnaye toured Ireland in the 1790s he noted that although Twiss had been treated unceremoniously by the Irish his celebrity had ensured excellent sales; not only of chamber pots, but also of his books, and even portraits.[9] Indeed if fame was not sufficient reward for his literary efforts, then Twiss might have been more sanguine on receiving news of his Irish sales figures. According to De Latocnaye, such was the commotion that a copy of his book 'could hardly be found in Dublin unsold.'[10] Twiss's *Tour in Ireland* went into three editions, plus translation, and booksellers were quick to replenish their supplies of *Travels through Portugal and Spain*; Twiss complained that a Dublin edition was 'incorrectly printed' and contained 'two bad prints'.[11] Yet his relationship with Dublin's print men was not overly sour. Twiss collaborated on a Dublin version of *A trip to Paris, in July and August, 1792*, providing it with additional paragraphs.[12] Other Irish men and women were more likely to remember him for reasons outside of his contribution to book sales, and Twiss felt that he was still being libelled as late as the 1790s; during the Union debates Pitt's 'gross insults' to the people of Ireland were compared to those of Twiss.[13] At the same time, while his literary reputation did not survive unimpaired, he was still worthy of citation and consultation. He was asked to contribute material for a planned 'zoology' of Ireland in 1789.[14]

The backlash against Twiss's *A tour in Ireland* also confirmed the maturity of Ireland's print culture, and, more broadly, its urban development. Tourists were quick to escape to the Irish countryside, but it was the urban world that gave them their profits, and awarded notoriety. Urban development, a 'renaissance' even, and the growth of the key elements of a public sphere – coffee houses, clubs, taverns, print culture, consumerism – played a vital part in Twiss's drubbing. A less sophisticated urban culture would surely have allowed his insults to pass unnoticed, unpublicized. It was therefore natural that future tourists like Bowden would be much more alive to the attractions of Irish town-life. At the same time Irish publishers were able to exploit the tour genre; not only in satire, but by personally commissioning travelogues, and even, as in the case of John Ferrar, publishing his own.[15]

The polarization of Irish society caused by the American War of Independence made 1776 a particularly inauspicious moment for Twiss to launch his attack upon Irish culture, manners and morals. Irish patriotism was becoming a more focused creed, with a coherent political programme, dominated by the quest for Free Trade and legislative independence. There is no doubt that *A tour in Ireland* became caught up in popular Dublin politics, and it is notable that Richard Lewis dedicated his *A defence of Ireland* to the patriot MP Sir Edward Newenham, while other works linked Twiss with unpopular Castle men like John Hely-Hutchinson and Sir John Blaquiere. Furthermore, although patriotism was very much an Anglican doctrine, the reaction to Twiss hinted at a much broader political 'nation' – Joep Leerssen refers to the controversy in the context of 'national pride'[16] – embracing not only literate Protestant men of the middling and upper orders, but also Catholics, women, and the lower sorts.

A side-swipe at Catholic 'old' Ireland was taken by the *Hibernian Journal* and other Dublin newspapers as a more general attack upon Irishness. The second performance of *The trip to Ireland; or, The tour writer* included 'St Patrick's Day in the Morning' in the overture, a tune once played by Irish soldiers fighting for France.[17] In his tour Twiss had backed Tobias Smollett's views on Irish myths of origin, and he saw contrary opinions as 'a heap of pedantic trash', which explains why Richard Lewis lauded Charles O'Conor, the Catholic antiquary, 'a True Friend to his country', and the most obvious champion of Gaelic Ireland.[18] Preston would echo this interest in Irish antiquities in his work for the *Press*.[19] Thus Twiss allowed the metropolitan Irish, and perhaps even selected tourists, to travel further down the road of rehabilitating former foes. The anti-Twiss reaction hinted at the embrace of the Gaelic Irish man, his culture and land; even 'old' Irish behaviour that looked like threatening Protestant politeness had value. Thus excessive hospitality, though in some ways reined in, was also rationalized and celebrated. Elsewhere the potato and whey became symbols of a nutritional diet, and in the case of the latter could be used as a means of attracting visitors to Ireland's burgeoning spa towns.

The brutish Connacht squire – whose religious identity is amorphous – was not only a useful fellow to have around in a brawl, but he was also an important reminder of the limits that should be put on the spread of fashionable modes. Sensible Irish masculinity offered a very useful contrast to effeminate macaroni manners. Happily the greatest period of fashionable excess in England coincided with an unrivalled period of Irish Protestant self-confidence. Tangible political victories were won by a nation in arms over a weakened British government, and for a short time this engendered a somewhat deluded sense of cultural superiority. The form of the Twiss backlash, seemingly a direct consequence of this, is worth emphasizing – and in particular its artificial, illusory nature. The involvement of Dublin's cash-conscious hacks and printers is one issue. Battle-lines were frequently crossed: Richard Lewis was happy to contribute a prologue to Gorges Howard's play *The female gamester* of 1778 and he wrote a playful poem defending the luckless author from his critics.[20] It is also clear that the anti-Twiss coalition contained many individuals happy with an old-whig approach to radicalism; men who would go on to support Protestant Ascendancy. Even so, at this precise point in Irish history the press could embrace the whole of Ireland in both a political and cultural sense. Just as Catholics were exhorted to take up arms and join the Volunteers, so the bluff, uncultivated and unspoiled Connacht squire was allowed to represent manly Ireland. Thus in Dublin's patriotic press he became the reluctant consumer of foreign goods and manners, gaining, in the words of Cornelius O'Dowde, 'excellent lessons concerning blowing my Nose, pairing my Nails' from *Chesterfield's Letters*; before reverting to type and beating Richard Twiss to a bloody pulp with a cudgel in a London alehouse.[21]

Notes

ABBREVIATIONS

BNL	*Belfast News-Letter*
Bodl.	Bodliean Library Oxford
BRO	Bedfordshire Record Office, Bedford
ECI	*Eighteenth-Century Ireland*
ESRO	East Sussex Record Office, Lewes
FDL	*Faulkner's Dublin Journal*
FLJ	*Finn's Leinster Journal*
FJ	*Freeman's Journal*
HC	*Hibernian Chronicle*
HJ	*Hibernian Journal*
HM	*Hibernian Magazine*
JRL	John Rylands Library, Manchester
LC	*Limerick Chronicle*
LJ	*Londonderry Journal*
MP	*Morning Post*
NLI	National Library of Ireland, Dublin
NLM	*New London Magazine*
SEP	*Saturday Evening Post*
SNL	*Saunders' News-Letter*
VEP	*Volunteer Evening Post*
WHM	*Walkers' Hibernian Magazine*

I. RICHARD TWISS'S *A TOUR IN IRELAND IN 1775*

1   Robinson to Nanny, 22 Mar. 1773 (BRO, L30/17/2/52)

2   *HM*, Aug. 1776, p. 550.

3   Glenn Hooper, *Travel writing and Ireland 1760–1860: culture history, politics* (Basingstoke, 2005), p. 12; Susan M. Kroeg, 'Philip Luckombe's *A tour through Ireland* (1780) and the problem of plagiarism', ECI, 19 (2004), p. 126.

4   *A tour in Ireland in 1775*: 'The private copy of the author Richard Twiss', p. 177 (NLI, MS 34251).

5   Katherine Turner, 'Twiss, Richard (1747–1821)', in *Oxford dictionary of national biography*; Joan K. Stemmler emphasizes the positive features of his

Iberian travelogue in 'An Anglo-Irish view of Spain: Richard Twiss's travels in Portugal and Spain in 1772 and 1773', *Dieciocho: Hispanic Enlightenment*, 23:2 (2000), pp 265–88.

6   Richard Twiss, *A trip to Paris, in July and August, 1792* (Dublin, 1793); David Rivers, *Literary memoirs of living authors of Great Britain* (2 vols, London, 1798), ii, 335.

7   Rivers, *Literary memoirs*, ii, 335.

8   James Boswell, *Life of Johnson*, ed. R.W. Chapman (Oxford, 1970), p. 614.

9   Heinrich Grellmann, *Dissertation on the gipsies*, trans. Matthew Raper (London, 1787), p. 168; NLM, Dec. 1788; Richard Twiss, *Miscellanies* (2 vols, London, 1805), i, i–x; Maria Edgeworth, *Belinda*, ed. Eiléan Ní Chuilleanáin (London, 1993), p. 103.

10 Richard Twiss, *A tour in Ireland in 1775. With a map, and a view of the salmon-leap at Ballyshannon* (London, 1776), p. 10.

11 Twiss, *Tour,* pp 39, 144.

12 John Harrington (ed.), *The English traveller in Ireland: English accounts of Ireland and the Irish since Elizabethan times* (Dublin, 1988); Andrew Hadfield and John McVeagh (eds), *Strangers to that land: British perceptions of Ireland from the Reformation to the Famine* (Gerrards Cross, 1994); Joep Leerssen, *Mere Irish and Fíor-Ghael: studies in the idea of Irish nationality, its development and literary expression prior to the nineteenth century* (Amsterdam, 1986); Martin Ryle, *Journeys in Ireland: literary travellers, rural landscapes, cultural relations* (Aldershot, 1999); Hooper, *Travel writing and Ireland; William H.A. Williams, Tourism, landscape, and the Irish character* (Madison, 2008).

13 Paul Hyland and James Kelly, 'Richard Twiss's *A tour of Ireland in 1775* (London, 1776): the missing pages and some other notes', *ECI,* 13 (1998), pp 53–64. Richard Twiss, *A tour in Ireland in 1775,* ed. Rachel Finnegan (Dublin, 2008).

2. IRISH TOURS AND TOURISTS

1 Quoted in William Zachs, *The first John Murray and the late eighteenth-century London book trade* (Oxford 1998), John Murray to John Gillies, 30 Sept. 1775.

2 Thomas Newenham, *A view of the natural, political and commercial circumstances of Ireland* (London, 1809), pp xvii, x–xi.

3 Arthur Young, *Tour in Ireland: with general observations on the present state of that kingdom* (2 vols, Dublin, 1780), i, xxiv.

4 Newenham, *A view,* p. xiii.

5 Zachs, *The first John Murray,* p. 204.

6 John Bush, *Hibernia curiosa: a letter from a gentleman in Dublin, to his friend at Dover in Kent,* (London, 1769), p. vii.

7 [William Chetwood], *A tour through Ireland. by two English gentlemen* (London, 1748); Thomas Campbell, *A philosophical survey of the south of Ireland* (Dublin, 1778); Philip Luckombe, *A tour through Ireland* (London, 1780).

8 Philip Luckombe, *The compleat Irish traveller* (London, 1788).

9 Mark Elstob, *A trip to Kilkenny, from Durham. by way of Whitehaven and Dublin in the year 1776* (Dublin, 1779); Twiss, private copy, pp 9, 14, 30, 36, 155.

10 Edward Du Bois, *My pocket book; or, Hints for a 'ryghte merrie and conceitede' tour, in quarto to be called 'The stranger in Ireland' in 1805* (London, 1808), p. 128.

11 Elstob, *Trip,* pp v–vi, 76–7, 154–7.

12 Luckombe, *Compleat,* p. xxii; John Carr, *The stranger in Ireland; or, A tour in the southern and western parts of that country in 1805,* intro. by Louis Cullen (Shannon, 1970), p. 409.

13 Twiss, *Tour,* p. 28; Samuel Derrick, *Letters written from Leverpoole, Chester, Cork, the lake of Killarney, Dublin, Tunbridge-Wells, and Bath* (2 vols, Dublin, 1767). See Percy Adams, *Travellers and travel liars, 1660–1800* (Berkeley, 1962).

14 *HM,* August 1776, p. 551.

15 Waddilove to Grantham, 7 Apr. 1775 (BRO, Lucas MSS L30/14/408/33)

16 *LJ,* 20 Sept. 1776; *FLJ,* 4–7 Sept. 1776.

17 Richard Lewis, *A defence of Ireland. A poem in answer to the partial and malicious accounts given of it by Mr Twiss, and other writers* (Dublin, 1776), p. 8; *FJ,* 27 Aug. 1776.

18 Young, *Tour,* i, xxviii.

19 Charles Topham Bowden, *A tour through Ireland* (Dublin, 1791), p. 237.

20 Derrick, *Letters,* i, 44, ii, 1–3.

21 John McVeagh (ed.), *Richard Pococke's Irish tours* (Dublin, 1995), pp 32, 71, 92.

22 *HM,* August 1776, p. 552.

23 *HJ,* 15–17 July 1776.

24 *FLJ,* 4–7 Sept. 1776.

25 *HM,* Aug. 1776, pp 551–2.

26 Johnson to Thrale, 12 May 1775 (Twiss, private copy, front page).

27 *An answer to a poetical epistle from Madam Teresa Pinna Ý Ruiz. By Richard Twiss, Esq. F.R.S. with notes by various hands* (Dublin, 1776), p. 12.

28 Fortescue to Caldwell, 12 Aug. 1775 (JRL, B3/10, vii, f139).

29 Twiss, *Tour*, p. 120.
30 Twiss to Douce, 15 May 1789 (Bodl., Douce MS D39, f19).
31 Twiss, *Tour*, pp 130, 150.
32 Twiss to Douce, 29 Jan. 1779 (Bodl., Douce MS D39, f1).
33 Twiss, private copy, pp 39, 137.
34 Ibid., pp 9, 142, back page, 177, 202.
35 Richard Twiss, *Travels through Portugal and Spain in 1772 and 1773* (London, 1775), p. 464; *SEP*, 28 Feb. 1824.
36 Young to Caldwell, 28 Jan. 1777 (JRL, B3/10, ix, f357).
37 Newenham, *A view*, pp x, xii; Bowden, *Tour*, p. 167.
38 Foster to Sheffield, 27 Feb. 1777 (ESRO, Sheffield MSS).
39 Young to Caldwell, 15 Nov. 1776 (JRL, B3/10 viii, f315).
40 *A month's tour in north Wales, Dublin and its environs, with observations upon their manners and police in the Year 1780* (London, 1781).
41 Campbell to Gough, 9 Feb. 1788 (Quoted in Clare O'Halloran, *Golden ages and barbarous nations: antiquarian debate and cultural politics in Ireland, c.1750–1800* (Cork, 2004), p. 65).
42 Constantia Maxwell, *The stranger in Ireland. From the reign of Elizabeth to the Great Famine* (London, 1954), p. 223; Williams, *Tourism, landscape*, p. 16; O'Halloran, *Golden ages*, pp 62, 66.
43 Richard Lewis, *The Dublin guide: or, A description of the city of Dublin* (Dublin, [1787]), p. ix.
44 Young to Caldwell, 28 Jan., 5 June 1777 (JRL, B3/10, ix, ff 357, 381–3).
45 Young to Caldwell, 12 July 1779 (JRL, B3/16, f413).
46 George Parker, *A view of society and manners in high and low life* (2 vols, London, 1781), i, 12–20.
47 Twiss to [Samuel Pratt], 24 Oct. 17[8]4 (Bodl., Montagu MSS D16); Twiss to Isaac D'Israeli, 20 March 1805 (Bodl., Hughenden MSS, ff 132–3).
48 Diary of a journey through England and Wales to Ireland made by Revd. J. Burrows, 1773 (NLI MSS 23,561, pp 65–72); Elstob, *Trip*, p. 79; Bowden, *Tour*, pp 1–2; E.D. Clarke, *A tour through the south of England, Wales, and part of Ireland, made during the summer of 1791* (London, 1792), p. 302; Carr, *Stranger*, p. 27.
49 *Pococke's Irish tours*, pp 98–9; *A general history of Ireland in its antient and modern state, on a new and concise plan. Collected by a gentleman*, (2 vols, Dublin, 1781), ii, 51; Bowden, *Tour*, p. 186.
50 Derrick, *Letters*, i, 66.
51 Elstob, *Trip*, p. 118, 136; *Pococke's Irish tours*, p. 100.
52 Burrows, 'Diary', pp 65–72; Parker, *A view*, ii, 97, 115; Elstob, *Trip*, pp 167–8.
53 Young, *Tour*, ii, 112; Carr, *Stranger*, p. 239.
54 Bowden, *Tour*, p. 25.
55 Clarke, *Tour*, p. 327; Bush, *Hibernia*, pp 160–1.
56 Derrick, *Letters*, i, 35.
57 Clarke, *Tour*, pp 326–7; Cooper, *Letters on the Irish nation: written during a visit to that kingdom, in the autumn of the year 1799* (London, 1800), pp 22–3.
58 Bush, *Hibernia*, pp 18–21.
59 Cooper, *Letters*, p. 21.
60 Carr, *Stranger*, p. 232; Bowden, *Tour*, p. 44.
61 Bush, *Hibernia*, pp 21–22, 26–7.
62 Ibid., p. 24; Luckombe, *Compleat*, p. 48; Carr, *Stranger*, p. 321.
63 Clarke, *Tour*, pp 305, 318.
64 *Two English gentlemen*, p. 82; Elstob, *Trip*, p. 92.
65 Young, *Tour*, i, 81–2; Elstob, *Trip*, p. 68; Sir Richard Colt Hoare, *Journal of a tour in Ireland, A.D.1806* (London, 1807), p. 306; Bowden, *Tour*, p. 191; Cooper, *Letters*, p. 112.
66 Campbell, *Philosophical survey*, p. 93; Parker, *A view*, ii, 99; *A month's tour*, p. 92; Luckombe, *Compleat*, p. 90; Cooper, *Letters*, p. 33; Carr, *Stranger*, p. 236.
67 Burrows, 'Diary', pp 46–7.
68 *A month's tour*, p. 109.
69 Burrows, 'Diary', pp 80–1, 93.
70 Young, *Tour in Ireland*, i, 5.
71 *A month's tour*, p. 109.
72 Elstob, *Trip*, pp 102–3; Hoare, *Journal*, p. 31.
73 Young, *Tour*, i, 113.
74 Campbell, *Philosophical survey*, p. 138.
75 *Pococke's Irish tours*, pp 65, 81–2; *A month's tour*, p. 75; Carr, *Stranger*, p. 154, 488; Twiss, *Tour*, p. 28; Luckombe, *Tour*, p. 39.
76 Bowden, *Tour*, p. 158; Carr, *Stranger*, p. 522; Newenham, *A view*, p. xvii.

77 Derrick, *Letters*, i, 46; Carr, *Stranger*, pp 151–2.
78 *A month's tour*, p. 76.
79 Clarke, *Tour*, p. 312.
80 Charles L. Batten, *Pleasurable instruction: form and convention in eighteenth-century travel literature* (Berkeley, 1978), p. 116.
81 Twiss, *Tour*, p. 73.
82 William Mavor, *The British tourists; or traveller's pocket companion, through England, Wales, Scotland, and Ireland* (6 vols, London, 1798–1800), ii, vii–viii.
83 Young to Caldwell, 22 Aug. 1776 (JRL, B3/10 viii, f279).
84 Bowden, *Tour*, p. 231.
85 Du Bois, *My pocket book*, p. 40.
86 *A month's tour*, pp 63–4.
87 Elstob, *Trip*, pp 98–101, 111.
88 *A month's tour*, pp 86, 97–99.
89 Clarke, *Tour*, pp. 305–6, 313–4, 329.
90 Carr, *Stranger*, pp 268–9; Maria Edgeworth, *Essay on Irish bulls* (1802) (Maria Edgeworth, *Tales and novels* (10 vols, London, 1893), iv, 152).
91 Carr, *Stranger*, pp 291, 99–100, v–ix; Maxwell, *Stranger in Ireland*, p. 237.

3. PUBLICATION AND POPULAR REACTION

1 *LJ*, 6 Sept. 1776.
2 *HJ*, 21–23 Aug. 1776.
3 *FDJ*, 13–15 Aug. 1776; *LJ*, 20 Aug., 1776; *HJ*, 23–5 Sept., 7–9 Oct., 20–2 Nov., 27–30 Dec. 1776.
4 *HJ*, 27–30 Dec. 1776.
5 *FJ*, 16–18 July, 1776; *HJ*, 22–4 July 1776; Lewis, *Defence*, p. 21.
6 *FJ*, 15 Oct. 1776, 5 June 1777.
7 *Poetical epistle*, p. 5.
8 [William Preston], *An heroic epistle from Donna Teresa Pinna y Ruiz, of Murcia, to Richard Twiss, Esq; F.R.S. with several explanatory notes, written by himself* (Dublin, 1776); [William Preston], *An heroic answer, from Richard Twiss, Esq. F.R.S. at Rotterdam, to Donna Teresa Pinna y Ruiz, of Murcia* (Dublin, 1776).
9 *HJ*, 23–6 Aug. 1776.
10 Twiss, private copy, p. 161.
11 Twiss to 'my wife', [nd] (Boldl., Phillipps-Robinson MSS C181).
12 [Preston], *Heroic epistle*, pp 18–20.
13 Robinson to Nanny, 29 March 1773 (BRO, Lucas MSS L30/17/2/53).
14 Grantham to Nanny, 5 April 1773 (BRO, Lucas MSS L30/17/4/49).
15 Robinson to Shelburne, 22 June 1779 (BRO, Lucas MSS L30/17/2/212).
16 Robinson to Nanny, 1 May 1775 (BRO, Lucas MSS L30/17/2/53).
17 Twiss to 'my wife', [nd] (Bodl., Phillipps-Robinson MSS C181).
18 Lewis, *Defence*, p. 13.
19 *HC*, 2–5 Sept. 1776; *FLJ*, 4–7 Sept. 1776.
20 *HC*, 25–29 July 1776; *BNL*, 6–10 Sept. 1776.
21 *FDJ*, 27–29 Aug. 1776.
22 *HJ*, 15–17 July 1776.
23 *Poetical epistle*, pp 5–9, 15.
24 *BNL*, 13–17 July 1776.
25 *FLJ*, 7–10 Aug. 1776.
26 *LC*, 1 July 1779.
27 *FDJ*, 2–4 July 1776; *SNL*, 8–10 July 1776.
28 *BNL*, 1–5 Aug. 1777; Lewis, *Dublin guide*, p. xi.
29 *HJ*, 21–23 Aug. 1776.
30 James Lackington, *Memoirs of the forty-five first years of the life of James Lackington written by himself* (London, 1794), p. 256; Rivers, *Literary memoirs*, ii, 335.
31 *FJ*, 10 October, 1776; Samuel Whyte, *Poems on various subjects* (Dublin, 1795), pp i–x.
32 Twiss, private copy, back page; *FJ*, 14 Sept. 1776.
33 Wynne to Caldwell, 13 Nov. 1777 (JRL, B3/10, ix, f448).
34 *HJ*, 7–10 Feb. 1777.
35 Twiss, private copy, title pages; Edgeworth, *Essay on Irish bulls*, p. 152.
36 Carr, *Stranger*, p. 101.
37 *The Bath contest* (Bath, 1769), p. 65.
38 *SNL*, 14–16 Aug. 1776; *FLJ*, 14–17 Aug. 1776; *FDJ*, 15–17 Aug. 1776, *LJ*, 20 August, 1776.
39 *HJ*, 12–14 Aug. 1776.
40 Ibid.
41 *FLJ*, 17–21 August, 1776.
42 *HJ*, 9–12 Aug. 1776.
43 Hyland and Kelly, 'Richard Twiss's *A tour of Ireland*', p. 56.
44 *BNL*, 10–13 Dec. 1776; *FLJ*, 4–7 Sept. 1776.

45 *BNL*, 10–13 Dec. 1776.
46 *HJ*, 23–26 Aug. 1776; *LJ*, 13 Sept. 1776.
47 *FLJ*, 28–31 Aug. 1776.
48 *HJ*, 7–9 Aug. 1776.
49 *HJ*, 23–25 Sept., 7–9 Oct., 25–27 Nov. 1776.
50 William Preston, *A congratulatory poem on the late successes of the British arms; particularly the triumphant evacuation of Boston* (Dublin, 1776).
51 Derrick, *Letters*, ii, 55.
52 Bush, *Hibernia*, pp 41–2; *A general history of Ireland*, ii. p. 121; William Hamilton, *Letters concerning the northern coast of the county of Antrim* (Dublin, 1786).
53 *A month's tour*, pp 85–6.
54 Twiss, private copy, p. 143.
55 *HJ*, 29–31 July 1776; Ben Johnson, *The sad shepherd: or, A tale of Robin Hood* (London, 1783), p. 220.
56 Mary Pollard, *A dictionary of members of the Dublin book trade, 1550–1800* (London, 2000), pp 409–10; *HJ*, 12–14 Aug. 1776.
57 Patrick Duigenan, *Lachrymæ academicæ; or, The present deplorable state of the College of the Holy and Undivided Trinity of Queen Elizabeth, near Dublin* (Dublin, 1777), p. 139.
58 *Poetical epistle*, p. 9, 6; *HJ*, 15–17 July 1776.
59 *Poetical epistle*, p. 9.
60 Ibid., pp 10, 13.
61 *HJ*, 13–16 Sept. 1776; *VEP*, 1–3 Jan. 1784.
62 *LJ*, 20 Sept. 1776.
63 *HJ*, 22–24 July 1776, 31 Jan.–3 Feb. 1777.
64 O'Halloran, *Golden ages*, p. 155; Young, *Tour*, i, 66; *A month's tour*, p. 61.
65 Bowden, *Tour*, pp 236–7; Carr, *Stranger*, p. 527.

4. TWISS AND IRISH CULTURAL LIFE

1 Twiss, *Tour*, p. 13; Campbell, *Philosophical survey*, p. 18.
2 Young, *Tour*, i, 17.
3 Burrows, 'Diary', p. 37; *A month's tour*, p. 30; *A general history*, i, 235.
4 Luckombe, *Compleat*, p. 33; Bowden, *Tour*, p. 5.
5 Elstob, *Trip*, p. 85; Luckombe, *Compleat*, p. 44; Bush, *Hibernia*, p. 12.
6 *Two English gentlemen*, pp 83–4; James Kelly, 'A tour in the south of Ireland in 1782', *North Munster Antiquarian Journal*, 29 (1987), p. 61; G. Holmes, *Sketches of some of the southern counties of Ireland* (London, 1801), pp 160–1.
7 *Pococke's Irish tours*, p. 96; Bowden, *Tour*, p. 168; Holmes, *Sketches*, p. 63; Carr, *Stranger*, p. 317.
8 Bush, *Hibernia*, p. 57; *Two English gentlemen*, p. 174; Luckombe, *Compleat*, p. 111.
9 Bowden, *Tour*, pp 149, 226–30, 245.
10 Peter Borsay, *The English urban renaissance: culture and society in the provincial town 1660–1770* (Oxford, 1989).
11 Twiss, *Tour*, pp 132–3, 136; Young, *Tour*, ii, 113.
12 Campbell, *Philosophical survey*, p. 205.
13 *A general history*, ii, 51; Bowden, *Tour*, p. 186.
14 Carr, *Stranger*, pp 116, 316; Bowden, *Tour*, p. 177.
15 *FLJ*, 4–7 Sept. 1776.
16 Frances Burney, *Evelina*, ed. Kristina Straub (Boston, 1997), p. 233.
17 Burrows, 'Diary', pp 46–8.
18 Young, *Tour*, i, 5.
19 Campbell, *Philosophical survey*, p. 31.
20 Carr, *Stranger*, p. 93; Bowden, *Tour*, p. 18.
21 Luckombe, *Compleat*, p. 46; Bush, *Hibernia*, p. 15–17.
22 Carr, *Stranger*, pp 230, 410–11; Topham Bowen, *Tour*, p. 42.
23 Carr, *Stranger*, pp 327, 317.
24 Burrows, 'Diary', pp 72–5.
25 Campbell, *Philosophical survey*, p. 40; Luckombe, *Compleat*, p. 50.
26 Twiss, *Tour*, p. 31; *HJ*, 12–14 Aug. 1776.
27 Burrows, 'Diary', pp 72–5.
28 Twiss, *Tour*, p. 31.
29 Ibid.
30 O'Conor to Faulkner, 15 Sept. 1767 (Robert E. Ward (ed.), *Prince of Dublin printers: the letters of George Faulkner* (Lexington, 1972), p. 99).
31 *Two English gentlemen*, pp 35, 94.
32 Elstob, *Trip*, p. 96.
33 Bowden, *Tour*, pp 65, 165, 182–3.
34 Twiss, private copy, pp 164–5.

35 Hyland and Kelly, 'Richard Twiss's *A tour of Ireland*', pp 57–8; Maria Edgeworth, *Castle Rackrent and Ennui*, ed. Marilyn Butler (London, 1992), pp. 325, 333.

36 *Poetical epistle*, p. 12.

37 Christopher Morash, *A history of Irish theatre, 1601–2000* (Cambridge, 2002), p. 54; *HJ*, 6–9 Feb. 1784.

38 *HJ*, 15–17 July 1776.

39 Twiss, *Tour*, p. 10.

40 *A month's tour*, p. 78; Bowden, *Tour*, p. 69.

41 Burrows, 'Diary', pp 72–5; *A month's tour*, p. 33.

42 H.M. Burke, *Riotous performances: the struggle for hegemony in the Irish theater, 1712–1784* (Notre Dame, 2003), p. 180.

43 Quoted in W.L. Pressly, *The life and art of James Barry* (New Haven, 1981), p. 84.

44 See Anne Crookshank, the Knight of Glin and William Laffan, *Masterpieces by Irish artists, 1660–1860* (London, 1999); William Laffan (ed.), *The sublime and the beautiful: Irish art, 1700–1830* (London, 2001).

45 *HJ*, 28–30 Aug. 1776.

46 Hooper, *Travel writing and Ireland*, pp 26–7.

47 Toby Barnard, *A new anatomy of Ireland: the Irish Protestants, 1649–1770* (New Haven, 2003), p. 291.

48 Twiss, *Tour*, p. 52.

49 Morash, *A history of Irish theatre*, p. 71.

50 Barnard, *A new anatomy of Ireland*, p. 291.

51 Bowden, *Tour*, p. 165.

52 *FLJ*, 4–7 Sept. 1776.

53 *HJ*, 7–9, 12–14 Aug. 1776.

54 Young, *Tour*, i, 104; Luckombe, *Compleat*, p. 125; Twiss, *Tour*, p. 142

5. THE PISS-POT TOURIST

1 Quoted in Robert Mahony, *Jonathan Swift: the Irish identity* (New Haven, 1995), p. 3.

2 *HJ*, 7–9 Aug. 1776.

3 *FDJ*, 8–10 Aug. 1776, *SNL*, 9–12 Aug. 1776; *FLJ*, 10–14 Aug. 1776.

4 Twiss, private copy, back page.

5 I am very grateful to Teresa Bolger for her thoughts on the shard of chamber pot.

6 *HJ*, 19–21 Aug. 1776.

7 *Poetical epistle*, p. 12

8 [Preston], *Heroic epistle*, p. 26; Jonathan Swift, *To the whole people of Ireland* (1724) (*The prose works of Jonathan Swift, vol. x, The Drapier's letters and other works 1724–1725*, ed. Herbert Davis (Oxford, 1941), p. 59).

9 *FJ*, 27 Aug. 1776; *WHM*, August 1776, p. 553.

10 William Preston, *The contrast: or, A comparison between the characters of the English and Irish in the Year 1780* (Dublin, 1780), pp 24–5.

11 Elstob, *Trip*, p. 101.

12 *HJ*, 12–14 Aug. 1776.

13 Carr, *Stranger*, p. 101.

14 *VEP*, 15–17 June 1784.

15 Quoted in Constantia Maxwell, *Dublin under the Georges, 1740–1830* (London, 1936), p. 276.

16 *HJ*, 16–19 Aug. 1776.

17 Young to Caldwell, 22 Aug. 1776 (JRL, B3/10, f279).

18 *BNL*, March 1777.

19 *LJ*, 13 Sept. 1776.

20 *HJ*, 4–6 Sept. 1776.

21 Quoted in Jae Num Lee, *Swift and scatological satire* (Alburquerque, 1971). p. 15.

22 Num Lee, *Swift and scatological satire*, p. 51.

23 Jonathan Swift, 'A character, panegyric, and description of the Legion Club' (Andrew Carpenter, *Verse in English from eighteenth-century Ireland* (Cork, 1998), p. 227).

24 Jonathan Swift, 'The gulph of all human possessions' (Jonathan Swift, *The complete poems*, ed. Pat Rogers (London, 1983), p. 307).

25 [Preston], *Heroic answer*, p. 10.

26 Num Lee, *Swift and scatological satire*, p. 84.

27 Thomas B. Gilmore, Jr, 'The comedy of Swift's scatological poems', *Publications of the Modern Languages Association of America*, 91:1 (1976), p. 37.

28 *FJ*, 31 Aug. 1776.

29 Mark Jenner, 'The roasting of the rump: scatology and the body politic

    in Restoration England', *Past and Present*, 177 (2002), p. 98.

30   *Poetical epistle*, p. 14.

31   Elstob, *Trip*, pp 98–9

32   Commonplace book of verses by Thomas Weekes, *c*.1775–77 (Wellcome Institute Library, MS 4985). I am very grateful to Dr Toby Barnard for this reference.

33   Num Lee, *Swift and scatological satire*, p. 90; Gilmore, Jr, 'Swift's scatological poems', p. 34.

34   *FJ*, 15 Oct., 14 Sept. 1776.

35   Num Lee, *Swift and scatological satire*, pp 65–6.

36   R.D.Y.C., *Fidéfract; an heroic poem. In four cantos. In the Hudibrastic style* (Dublin, 1778), pp 34–5.

37   See Robert Adams Day, Sex, scatology, Smollett', in Paul-Gabriel Boucé (ed.), *Sexuality in eighteenth-century Britain* (Manchester, 1982), p. 229.

38   *FLJ*, 14–17 August 1776.

39   *FJ*, 31 Aug. 1776.

40   Quoted in Roy Porter, 'Consumption: disease of the consumer society?', in Roy Porter and John Brewer (eds), *Consumption and the world of goods* (London, 1994), p. 61.

41   *FJ*, 31 Aug., 14 Sept. 1776; Henry Carey, *Chrononhotonthologos* (London, 1800), p. 13.

42   *Poetical epistle*, p. 16.

43   Luckombe, *Tour*, p. 17.

44   Quoted in Hyland and Kelly, 'Richard Twiss's *A tour of Ireland*', p. 61.

45   John Cozine, *Dick Twiss* (New York, 1780) pp 6–7; *Atheneum*, 15 Dec. 1821; *New-York Mirror*, 6 Mar. 1824; *SEP*, 28 Feb. 1824.

46   Luckombe, *Tour*, p. 17.

47   Francis Grose, *A classical dictionary of the vulgar tongue* (London, 1805).

48   Robert Jephson, *The confessions of James Baptise Couteau, citizen of France, written by himself* (2 vols, London, 1794), ii, 208–10; [Preston], *Heroic epistle*, p. 17.

49   Num Lee, *Swift and scatological satire*, p. 93.

50   Grose, *Dictionary*.

51   *HJ*, 9–11 Sept. 1776.

52   *Poetical epistle*, p. 9.

53   *VEP*, 19–21 Feb. 1784.

54   Maurice Craig, *Dublin, 1660–1800* (Dublin, 1969), p. 210.

55   M.H. Thuente, '"The Belfast laugh": the context and significance of United Irish satires' in Jim Smyth (ed.), *Revolution, counter-revolution and union: Ireland in the 1790s* (Cambridge, 2000), p. 81.

6. TWISS AND THE FORMATION OF IRISH IDENTITY

1   See Williams, *Tourism, landscape*, p. 7.

2   Bowden, *Tour*, p. 187.

3   Twiss, *Tour*, p. 136.

4   Philip Carter, *Men and the emergence of polite society, Britain, 1660–1800* (London, 2001), p. 151.

5   See James Kelly, 'That damn'd thing called honour': duelling in Ireland, 1570–1860* (Cork, 1995).

6   Twiss, *A Tour*, p. 9; *Hibernian Journal*, 12–14 Aug. 1776.

7   Twiss, *Travels through Portugal*, pp 62, 167, 223–4.

8   Waddilove to Grantham, 7 April 1775 (BRO, Lucas MS 30/14/408/33).

9   Lewis, *Defence*, pp 10, 12.

10   *HJ*, 24–26 July 1776; *FLJ*, 4–7 Sept. 1776.

11   *WHM*, August 1776, p. 552; *HJ*, 23–6 Aug. 1776.

12   *FJ*, 27 Aug. 1776.

13   [Preston], *Heroic epistle*, p. 18n.

14   Twiss, *A tour*, p. 54.

15   D.M. Weed, 'Sexual positions: men of pleasure, economy, and dignity in Boswell's *London Journal*', *Eighteenth-Century Studies*, 31 (1997–8), p. 216.

16   Lewis, *Defence*, p. 12.

17   Kathleen Wilson, *The island race: Englishness, empire and gender in the eighteenth century* (London, 2003), p. 50.

18   *BNL*, 22 Mar. 1754; Vincent Morley, *Irish opinion and the American Revolution, 1760–1783* (Cambridge, 2002), p. 27.

19   Kathleen Wilson, *Sense of the people: politics, culture and imperialism in England, 1715–1785* (Cambridge, 1995), p. 220; Preston, *Congratulatory poem*, p. 13.

20   Lewis, *Defence*, pp 9, 28.

21   *BNL*, 14–17 Apr. 1778.

22   *HJ*, 16–19 Aug., 11–13 Sept. 1776.

23 *HJ*, 28–30 Aug. 1776.
24 Twiss, *Tour*, p. 177; Lewis, *Defence*, p. 18.
25 *HJ*, 6–8 Jan., 10–13 Jan. 1777.
26 *HJ*, 24–27 Jan. 1777.
27 Bush, *Hibernia*, p. 27.
28 *HJ*, 22–24 July 1776.
29 *FLJ*, 4–7 Sept. 1776.
30 Lewis, *Defence*, p. 22.
31 [Preston], *Heroic answer*, p. 8.
32 *HJ*., 24–26, 29–31 July 1776.
33 *FLJ*, 4–7 Sept. 1776.
34 *HJ*, 24–26 July 1776.
35 *HJ*, 16–19, 23–26 Aug. 1776.
36 [Preston], *Heroic answer*, p. 12.
37 Burke, *Riotous performances*, pp 132–3.
38 Burrows, 'Diary', p. 6.
39 O'Halloran, *Golden ages*, p. 97.
40 *HJ*, 7–9 Aug. 1776.
41 *HJ*, 11–13 Sept. 1776.
42 *BNL*, 16–20 July 1790.
43 Twiss to Douce, 24 July, 4 Aug. 1790 (Bodl., Douce MSS, d. 39, ff21–3); *Times*, 20 July 1790.
44 Twiss to Douce, 6 Aug., 17 Sept. 1792 (Bodl., Douce MSS, d. 39, ff44–6); Twiss to Douce, [nd], (Bodl., Douce MSS, d. 39, f113).
45 Twiss, private copy; *MP*, 20 Feb. 1799.
46 [Preston], *Heroic answer*, p. 11.
47 Twiss, *Tour*, pp 49–50; Bowden, *Tour*, p. 191.
48 [Preston], *Heroic answer*, p. 20.
49 Twiss, *Tour*, p. 30.
50 Twiss, private copy, p. 74.
51 *HJ*, 12–14 Aug. 1776.
52 Burrows, 'Diary', pp 80–1.
53 Carole Fabricant, 'Colonial sublimities and sublimations: Swift, Burke, and Ireland', *English Literary History*, 72 (2005), p. 321; Jonathan Swift, *A short view of the state of Ireland* (Dublin, 1727–8) (*Prose works*, xii, 10).
54 Fabricant, 'Colonial Sublimities', pp 321–2.
55 Twiss, *Tour*, p. 30.
56 Maria Edgeworth, *Castle Rackrent and Ennui*, ed. Marilyn Butler (London, 1992), pp 210–11.
57 Carr, *Stranger*, pp 268–9.
58 Gamble to Caldwell, 3 Oct. 1776 (JRL, B3/10, viii, f309).
59 W.H.G. Bagshawe, *The Bagshawes of Ford: a biographical pedigree* (London, 1886), pp 324–6.
60 [Preston], *Heroic answer*, p. 16; *HJ*, 24–6 July 1776.
61 Edgeworth, *Castle Rackrent and Ennui*, p. 210.
62 *FLJ*, 4–7 Sept. 1776.
63 *HM*, August 1777, p. 550.
64 Jephson, *Confessions*, ii, 210–11.
65 *HJ*, 28–30 Aug., 1776, 17–19 Feb. 1777, 18–21 Oct. 1776, 21–24 March 1777; *A month's tour*, p. 39.
66 Preston, *Congratulatory poem*, pp 6–9; William Preston, *The female congress; or, the temple of Cotytto: A mock heroic poem, in four cantos* (London, 1779), p. 33.
67 *Fidéfract*, pp 16, 30.
68 Ibid., p. 34.
69 *HJ*, 9–11 Oct. 1776.
70 Bowden, *Tour*, p. 21.
71 *HM*, August 1776, p. 553.
72 *LJ*, 20 Sept. 1776; *BNL*, 10–13 Dec. 1776.
73 Twiss, *Tour*, p. 8.
74 Ibid., p. 37.
75 See for example Williams, *Tourism, Landscape*, pp 93–4.
76 Seamus Deane, *Celtic revivals: essays in modern Irish literature, 1880–1980* (London, 1985), p. 20.
77 *WHM*, August 1776.
78 *FDJ*, 31 Oct.-2 Nov. 1776.
79 Bowden, *Tour*, p. 163.
80 *LJ*, 3 Sept. 1776.
81 James Kelly, '"Glorious and Immortal Memory": commemoration and Protestant identity in Ireland 1660–1800', *Proceedings of the Royal Irish Academy*, 94C (1994), pp 44–5.
82 *HJ*, 27–30 Dec. 1776, 10–13 Jan. 1777, 31 Jan. 1776–3 Feb. 1777.

7. CONCLUSION

1 *Loyal volunteers of London & environs infantry & cavalry, in their respective uniforms* ([London, 1799]), no. xvii; O'Halloran, *Golden ages*, p. 62.
2 Twiss, private copy, p. 143.
3 Jephson, *Confessions*, ii, 210.
4 Richard Twiss, *A trip to Paris in July and August, 1792* (Dublin, 1793), pp 158–9.
5 Bush, *Hibernia*, pp ix–x.

---

6 Robinson to Nanny, 30 Oct. 1774 (BRO, Lucas MSS, L30/17/2/125).

7 Kelly, 'A tour in the South', p. 61.

8 *HJ*, 22–24 July 1776.

9 *HC*, July 1776.

10 De Latocnaye, *A Frenchman's Walk Through Ireland 1796–7*, trans. by J. Stevenson (Belfast, 1984), p. 22.

11 *FLJ*, 27–31 July, 7–10 Aug. 1776; *SNL*, 21–23 Aug., 16–18 Sept. 1776.

12 Twiss, *Miscellanies*, ii, 392.

13 Twiss to Douce, 24 July 1790 (Bodl., Douce MSS D39, f21); *MP*, 20 Feb. 1799.

14 Twiss to Douce, 22 May 1789 (Bodl., Douce MSS d. 39, f15).

15 John Ferrar, *A tour from Dublin to London, in 1795* (Dublin, 1796).

16 Leerssen, *Mere Irish and Fíor-Ghael*, p. 409.

17 *HJ*, 21–4 Feb. 1777.

18 Twiss, *Tour*, p. 151; Lewis, *Defence*, p. 27.

19 Norman Vance, 'Celts, Carthaginians and constitutions: Anglo-Irish literary relations, 1780–1820', *Irish Historical Studies*, 86 (1980), p. 223.

20 Gorges Edmond Howard, *The miscellaneous works, in verse and prose* (3 vols, Dublin, 1782), i, cclvii; ibid., iii, 346.

21 *HJ*, 31 Jan. 1776–3, Feb. 1777.